Language in
Mathematics

Language in Mathematics

Edited by
Jennie Bickmore-Brand

HEINEMANN
Portsmouth, NH

Heinemann
A division of Reed Publishing (USA), Inc.
361 Hanover Street, Portsmouth, NH 03801-3912
Offices and agents throughout the world

©1990 Australian Reading Association
P.O Box 78
Carlton South, Victoria 3053 Australia

First U.S. Printing 1993
ISBN 0-435-08340-6 (Heinemann)

Library of Congress Cataloging-in-Publication Data

Language in mathematics / edited by Jennie Bickmore-Brand.
    p. cm.
    Originally published: Perth: Australian Reading Association, 1990.
    ISBN 0-435-08340-6
    1. Mathematics—Study and teaching (Primary)—Australia.
2. Language and education—Australia. I. Bickmore-Brand, Jennie.
QA135.5.L26 1993
372.7'044—dc20   92-46790
                                                                      CIP

Cover art by Mary Tsagdouris
LaserSet by N.S Hudson Publishing Services, Hawthorn

Printed in the United States of America on Acid Free Paper
93 94 95 96 97 9 8 7 6 5 4 3 2 1

Contents

Acknowledgements

I am indebted to Bruce Shortland-Jones whose advice and assistance were significant to the initial concept of the book.

Foreword

I believe this book is timely for two reasons. Firstly because it is International Literacy Year and all society is becoming aware of the multiplicity of language demands people need in order to function in today's society. Secondly because there seems to be a general disillusionment about what constitutes the fundamentals of integrating mathematics into a language program. Across Australia, teachers are dabbling with how to mesh mathematical concepts into programs and yet stay true to the rigours of the mathematical discipline.

Teachers have been enthused by the new stream of picture books from progressive publishing companies and authors, where integration seems obvious. We have Base, Anno, Carle and Hutchins to thank for starting this trend. *Counting on Frank* by R. Clement (Collins) is a must for teaching estimation! These teachers are enjoying the new context in which mathematics can lie.

Other teachers have gone down a much more metacognitive path for developing mathematical concepts. These teachers have seen the power of process-writing techniques in getting children to be reflective and analytical, and to share their growing mathematical formulations.

Still others have looked at the traditional content being provided by syllabi and see 'challenges' or open-ended questions as the stimulus for meaningful investigations by children.

Yet regardless of the injections that teachers are trying to give their mathematical programs, mathematics continues to have a very poor profile in our society. This is exhibited by the low retention rates of students electing to study mathematics in secondary and tertiary studies, and the perception by the majority of students and teachers that mathematics is 'hard'. Similarly there is a general attitude by adults that they're not very good at mathematics.

Professor John Mack of the Department of Mathematics, University of Sydney challenged Directors, Principals and teachers to consider why they should retain mathematics in their curriculum in the 21st century. He considers that schools have lost sight of the community context from which mathematics has arisen:

> *By and large, [students] grow up believing quite firmly that school mathematics is something done in school that has no relationship with the rest of the world, and is certainly not anything needed for the rest of their lives.*

This book is therefore my response to Professor John Mack, and a challenge to teachers to make mathematics learning relevant and lasting. I have contributed two theoretical papers to this book which provide an underlying confidence in the recurring themes emerging in the more practical papers. Gawned's attempt to generate a framework for integrating language with mathematical learning is an ambitious task. Her model represents the backdrop for future discussion in this whole area. The credibility of the model is actualised by the teachers at the Carawatha Language Development Centre, whose paper explicitly seeks to reflect on the model in a school context. Unwittingly Waters and Montgomery, from the other side of the continent, have incorporated the spirit of the Gawned model into their own classroom practice across the grade levels. Similarly Stoessiger and Edmunds in Tasmania are working on the application of a theoretical language base to mathematical learning. MacGregor reminds of the reality that classrooms are full of learners with very different prior knowledge, making any joint construction of meaning in the mathematical register very complex. Reeves contributes to the emphasis found throughout the book, that the language used to process and express mathematical ideas needs to have a high profile in classrooms.

Regardless of the direction future research takes in this area of language and mathematics, it is apparent from this book that some common valuable themes are emerging for education. I trust that this book has provided a new context for language and mathematics which will encourage classroom practitioners to reflect upon their practices.

Jennie Bickmore-Brand
(Editor)

About the authors

Jennie Bickmore-Brand lectures at Curtin University in Education and has recently completed her Masters Degree in Language and Mathematics. The chapters here represent significant reference to that research. Jennie was co-convenor for the Western Australian State Literacy Conference in May 1990, and has an interest in the accessibility of genres in society, in particular the mathematics register.

Sue Gawned has just completed a position as Acting Assistant Principal Speech Pathologist in the Health Department of WA., and clinical supervisor in the Speech and Hearing Science Department, Curtin University. Her interests include child language development and the relationship between language and learning.

The Carawatha Language Development Centre WA (Principal, Marie Donovan) is classified as a Special School. It caters for children who have academic, emotional and social performance below average, due to profound neurological language delay/disorder. The staff chose to research the language of problem-solving, activity specific language, the language of mathematics curriculum and literacy in mathematics.

Noelene Reeves is Superintendent of Education, Melville District for the Ministry of Education, Western Australia. Her interests include the relationship of mathematical development and language development, conceptual development, and how children process symbolic information.

Mark Waters and **Pam Montgomery** are both primary teachers working to draw inferences from language research for providing an early learning environment conducive to learning mathematics. Both writers are doing their Masters through Deakin University in this field of language and mathematics. At Strathbogie School they have replicated features of the early learning environment within the mathematics classroom. Children from Years Prep through to Six are able to continue their natural explorations of number, pattern, shape and measurement.

Mark is currently working at Tatong Primary School, a three-teacher school in Victoria.

Pam is Head of Cheshunt Primary School, a two-teacher school in Victoria.

Helen Pengelly is a lecturer in Mathematics Education in the School of Education S.A.C.A.E. Magill site. Her interests include the development of children's understanding and use of symbolic representation in mathematics, and the linguistic and cognitive processes children engage in to construct meaning.

Mollie MacGregor lectures at the University of Melbourne in Mathematics Education. She recently completed her Ph.D. in children's understanding and use of mathematical language and how the difficulties children experience, particularly E.S.L. children, are related to their linguistic abilities.

Joy Edmunds is currently a Kindergarten to Year 8 Curriculum Officer in Mathematics for the Education Department Curriculum Development and Evaluation Section. She also lectures at the University of Tasmania in Early Childhood mathematics.

Rex Stoessiger has his Doctorate in Chemistry and is currently a Senior Education Officer in Professional Development at the Centre for Advanced Teaching in Tasmania.

Joy and Rex have been exploring action research with groups of teachers around Tasmania and trialling problem-solving techniques.

1

Implications from recent research in
language arts for mathematical teaching

Jennie Bickmore-Brand

Bickmore-Brand summarises the current research into the area of language arts from the many disciplines which continue to influence the field. She extracted common themes or 'strands' which emerged from this literature search to investigate their possible application to mathematical teaching and learning. This paper takes one of the strands only and develops it – that of creating a meaningful context for learning. Mathematics is regarded as the most complex of the abstract systems. It can only offer decontextualised activities for children to process once they have been immersed in enough whole and relevant examples that they can progressively self-generate the rules, leading to less concrete application. For this to be effective Bickmore-Brand has support from research which directs teachers to be aware of the socio-cultural context in which the child is capable of functioning.

Discussions about school mathematics often elicit strong feelings since few adults complete schooling with neutral attitudes towards mathematics. For too many Australians, learning mathematics at school is not intellectually stimulating nor emotionally satisfying, but a frustrating experience.

Senator Susan Ryan (*Bloom*, 1986, p. 6)

This paper is a section from a much larger interpretive literature search into the language arts field (Bickmore-Brand 1989). The study emerged because I believed there were many useful innovations in the way literacy was being taught in school, particularly in the past ten years, which could be applied to mathematics classrooms.

I selected the following major disciplines which had influenced and continue to influence the language arts field and how teachers operate in classrooms: socio-psycholinguistic theory, language and learning theories, metacognition theory, literacy learning theory, educational psychology theories and early childhood learning theories. I read the key contributors within each discipline and began to draw up an extensive list of common themes that seemed to be emerging.

Inevitably, with such a huge amount of resources, many themes emerged, some of which were barely consistent across all the disciplines and others which were dominant in several but did not have relevance across the board. The resulting themes, or 'strands' as I call them in this paper, represent the most consistent, and those which I believe offer the most for the practising classroom teacher.

These 'strands' are:
- 'context' – creating a meaningful and relevant context for the transmission of knowledge, skills and values;
- 'interest' – realising the starting point for learning must be from the knowledge, skills and or values base of the learner;
- 'modelling' – providing opportunities to see the knowledge, skills and/ or values in operation by a 'significant' person;
- 'scaffolding' – challenging children to go beyond their current thinking, continually increasing their capacities;
- 'metacognition' – making explicit the learning processes which are occurring in the classroom;
- 'responsibility' – developing in children the capacity to accept increasingly more responsibility for their learning;
- 'community' – creating a supportive classroom environment where children feel free to take risks and be part of a shared context.

While each of these themes has been developed in detail in terms of the research from which each is based and their application to mathematics, the most powerful single message is embodied in the first strand – 'context'. Space does not permit me to do justice to the other strands but it is hoped that by inspecting this strand the reader will be inspired to follow up the remaining information.

Creating a meaningful context for learning

The premise behind the context strand is that most learning occurs naturally within a context which makes the value of the learning obvious to the learner and motivates the learner to acquire the skill. The natural language learning exponents advocate the need for wholistic contexts for skills development (see the works of Goodman (1983), Cambourne (1988), Holdaway (1986), Smith (1988)).

Professor John Mack of the Department of Mathematics, University of Sydney (1988, cited in Pengelly 1988) challenged Directors, Principals and teachers to consider why they should retain mathematics in their curriculum in the 21st century. He considers that schools have lost sight of the community context from which mathematics has arisen:

> *By and large, they grow up believing quite firmly that school mathematics is something done in school that has no relationship with the rest of the world, and is certainly not anything needed for the rest of their lives.*
>
> (Pengelly, 1988, pp. 4–5)

Immersion in whole contexts

What is being indicated is the difficulty of mathematics teaching where the mathematical activities required of children in the classroom are predominantly decontextualised in nature. What can be learned from language learning research, particularly in the area of reading, is the capacity of the readers to refine their ability to cope with decontextualised situations providing they first have been immersed in print presented in whole contexts that are relevant and meaningful to them.

Mathematics has historically preoccupied itself with progressively moving students through a series of isolated subskills activities, which has streamlined their textbooks and mathematics instruction. Recent research (Clements 1987, and especially that of Newman (1988) who has worked with children in their grasping of computer technology), has noted that the learner needs to have a global vision roughly in mind before attempting the minor details. That is, the learner needs to get a sense of the broader context that the skills fit into.

Many schools across Australia are now attempting to respond to this as they employ the practice of Cambourne (1986) and apply his learning condition of 'immersion' to their mathematics classrooms. However, others before him, namely Holdaway (1979) and Smith (1988) have contributed considerable research which lauds this capacity of the individual to self-generate the rules of language of the culture in which they have been immersed.

Goodman (1983) reminds us of the strategies children employ when handling print; prediction, using background knowledge, confirmation or selection of more cues to make predictions, and then confirmation. Context is paramount to the construction of meaning the whole way through. It is the backdrop against which the parts have to make sense.

Contexts therefore do have relevance for mathematics learning in classrooms: not only because there is a lot of reading in mathematics, but because this highlights the natural strategy that children employ to make sense of their world.

Chartres (1988) recommends that teachers need to assist children to develop connections between the mathematical ideas, skills and processes being taught in school with their own developing construction of the world (see also 'interest' strand). Effort needs to be put into the problems found in mathematics textbooks because at the moment students can no longer rely on their natural screening device of meaning. They have become more random in their guessing, and hope for success rather than have it confirmed internally by sense.

Clearly, mathematics is one of the most complex of the abstract systems the child will have to master, as Donaldson (1979) shows.

> *Children need to see mathematical language in its conceptual context and gradually come to recognise it in less supported contexts. So the first step is the step of conceptualising language – becoming aware of it as a separate structure, freeing it from its embeddedness in events.*
> (Donaldson, 1979)

Communicating understanding

Children frequently display the ability to use language appropriately in context but when asked to define it they often cannot (this notion is explored further in the 'metacognition' strand).

> *Using language appropriately in a common, real experience setting is much easier than defining a term or explaining what something is in the abstract.*
> (Cambourne, 1988, p. 73)

Children need to be given opportunities to explore mathematical relationships before they should be expected to write mathematics (Pengelly 1986, p. 16). Children's ability to demonstrate what they have learned is not always consistent with what they know (Clements and Del Campo 1987):

> *Children's expressive understandings of fractions are not as strong as their receptive understandings. In other words, despite the fact that children sometimes appear to have understood mathematical ideas which have been communicated to them, often they cannot communicate these same ideas to others (or even to themselves). (p. 27)*

It is suggested that children need ample opportunity to do mathematics in a variety of modes – drawing, speaking – in the form of discussing, comparing and reflecting, dramatising, performing, writing and imaging, in a risk-free environment (see also 'community' strand). This represents a shift from the traditionally receptive mode of children, listening and reading and undergoing restrictive writing experiences, to one utilising more of a balance by introducing more expressive opportunities.

The purpose behind this shift is twofold. Firstly it enables the teachers a broader range of signs on which to judge the child's understanding. Secondly, because the expressive mode is being produced by the child it will be based on their experiences and cognitive structures. This means that real-life experiences within the child's cognitive structures will be brought to bear upon the tasks provided by the school learning environment.

The strength of these learning procedures as described by Clements and Del Campo (1987) lie in their contextualised nature. The authors recommend not only mental and verbal images of operations being created but encourage actual recall of episodes where objects were manipulated as the result of an operation being used in a context. This provides a firm base in which the concept or operation can be attached to the child's schema (p. 32).

Setting up for independence

Gray (1987) is suggesting that we consider 'mathematical operations as constituting elements of texts which are representative of particular mathematical genres' (Gray 1987, p. 16). Different social contexts have mathematical operations or concepts embedded in them and these need to be raised with the children in such a way that they come to identify with the new context as being relevant to their own lives.

Consequently we need to pitch our teaching not at the concept nor the child 'alone' but to include the social context in which the child is capable of functioning with that concept, initially with adult support (Gray 1987, p. 13). This is reminiscent of Cazden (1983), who comments on the role adults play in setting up support for the learning of the model, which is set within an experience before the teacher or adult gradually increases the level of decontextualising of the model so that the underlying structure is what is acquired, and not just the imitations of the examples (see 'scaffolding' strand).

This has implications for mathematics teaching in that the concept or operation in the first instance should be highly teacher and context supported and the process of decontextualisation should be done gradually and in an environment where children feel they can take the risks (see 'community' strand). In order to achieve this, various problem-solving environments would need to be set up. Similarly schools would need to have rituals which tap into the important mathematical texts which children need to master in order to function in their culture. Learning these would become part of the child's socialising; that is, the child would have mastered another genre and its accompanying concepts and operations on which to call as needed.

There would need to be not only contextual but also predictive components, so the children may grasp the model as a reference for future text situations. Even within these rituals the teacher does not want rote learning of the model but rather wishes to generate a model together with the children in such a way that the learners would eventually construct the concept and operations for themselves. The text routines may well be obvious, as there is a selection of contexts that have been socially negotiated, but children need to negotiate their goals so that they can be in a position of making choices in their construction of meaning i.e. to enable them to keep the operations relevant to their needs. It is desirable that they be wholly involved, and that this should not be at a rote learning level (Athey 1983).

Relevance

Holdaway (1986) notes that in most classroom contexts, particularly so in mathematics classrooms, the teacher demonstrates for the benefit of the learners rather than out of any real use of the skill for their own life's functioning. He is emphatic that learning be presented as whole and in relevant contexts:

> *The emphasis of the model on the sharing of authentic skill implies that it will be the actual content and strategies of literacy which will be emulated – not some apparently logical progression of non-authentic sub-skills. Literacy, as it is learned, will not be turned into rules, or even into a game, but will display a serious and genuine practice of literate acts.*
>
> (Holdaway 1986, p. 63)

Teachers of mathematics are renowned for their modelling of favourite strategies (Galbraith 1987). They do, however, need to have expression in real world contexts, and much more permanent learning occurs if the strategies have been generated by the learners themselves (Piaget 1973, p. 93. See also the generating own rules section in 'interest' strand, and 'modelling' strand). Teachers should be encouraged to use the environment around them as a resource for mathematics rather than use only the text book examples. The dilemma is that

> ...*most primary school teachers have little experience of mathematics outside school mathematics ...*
>
> (Pengelly, 1988, pp. 4–5)

Boomer (1988) has done extensive work concerning the benefits of using real contexts for learning and the importance of concepts being taught within a context which can be transferred to other contexts. He sees the need to change mathematics to be more 'relational' (Skemp 1977) or 'action knowledge' (Barnes 1976) where the students so understand the underlying principles of what they are learning that they can reapply them to solve problems in different contexts. This, after all, is the true test of any valuable knowledge; that it be viable/transferable in a variety of contexts (see von Glaserfeld, 1983).

Implications

To summarise then, language has its existence because of its context. It therefore becomes important to establish in classrooms where the mathematical language/terminology embodies contexts which are different from those the child has become used to. This is particularly important when a child starts formal education; the teacher needs to find out the child's existing perception of the concept behind the language, and then modify it for the school's purposes if necessary.

The 'context' strand recognises as a feature of mathematics genres that they are largely decontextualised, and that in order for children to assimilate the concepts embedded in these mathematical texts the teacher must start where the child is at. The teacher will need to jointly reconstruct a situation where the new concept can be used in a way that is relevant to the child, and together they can generate the underlying rule which accompanies that concept or operation. Later, with a gradual release of the scaffolding and subsequent context, the child will be in a position to comprehend and operate within that genre at a more abstract level. Mathematics can only present decontextualised problems/exercises when the student has been sufficiently immersed in similar problems within a context, to the point from which the student is able to gradually have the context less specified and finally to cope with the decontextualised problem.

Hence what is being recommended is the integration of skills in the mind of the learner, which can only occur if the learner, when working on the separate skills, has the overall context and its relevance to her/

his life's functioning quite clear as a motivational component to learning.

I believe there has been a breakdown in communication with students not getting the message or making the meaning that their teachers wished for them. We need to look at the language that underpins the transmission of the knowledge, and hence need to give consideration to the extrapolation from those researchers in the language field, and apply their insights to communication in mathematics.

References

Athey, I. (1983) 'Thinking and Experience: The Cognitive Base for Language Experience' in Parker, R. & Davis, F. *Developing Literacy: Young Children's Use of Language* International Reading Association, Newark, Delaware.

Barnes, D (1992) *From Communication to Curriculum* Portsmouth, NH: Boyton/Cook.

Bickmore-Brand, J. (1989) 'What can be learned from recent research in Language Arts that can be applied to Mathematical Teaching' unpublished dissertation, Deakin University.

Bloom, W. (1986) 'The relevance of the school mathematics curriculum' in *The Australian Mathematics Teacher 42*, 4 (Dec) pp. 6–7.

Boomer, G. (1988) 'From Catechism to Communication: Language Learning and Mathematics' in *Australian Mathematics Teacher 42*, 1 (April).

Cambourne, B. (1986) 'Rediscovering natural literacy learning; old wine in a new bottle'. Paper presented at the ESL Conference Singapore, April, mimeograph.

Cambourne, B. (1988) *The Whole Story: Natural Learning and Acquisition of Literacy in the Classroom* Ashton Scholastic, Gosford, New Zealand.

Cazden, C.B. (1983) 'Adult Assistance to Language Development: Scaffolds, Models, and Direct Instruction' in Parker, R. & Davis, F.A. (Eds) *Developing Literacy: Young Children's Use of Language*, International Reading Association, Newark, Delaware.

Chartres, M. (1988) 'What is Mathematics? A Personal Perspective in *The Australian Mathematics Teacher 44*, 3 (Oct).

Clements, M.A., & Del Campo, G. (1987) *Manual for the professional development of teachers of beginning mathematicians* Association of Independent Schools of Victoria/Catholic Education Office of Victoria, Melbourne.

Donaldson, M (1979) *Children's Minds* New York: Norton.

Galbraith, P. (1987) 'Modelling – Teaching Modelling' in *The Australian Mathematics Teacher 43*, 4 (Dec).

Goodman, Y. (1983) 'Beginning Reading Development: strategies and principles' in Parker, R. & Davis, F. *Developing Literacy: Young Children's Use of Language* International Reading Association, Newark, Delaware.

Gray, B. (1987) 'How Natural is Natural Language Teaching – Employing Wholistic Methodology in the Classroom' in *Australian Journal of Early Childhood 12*, 4 (Dec).

Holdaway, D. (1979) *Foundations of Literacy Portsmouth*, NH: Heinemann.

Holdaway, D. (1986) 'The Structure of Natural Learning as a Basis for Literacy Instruction' in *The Pursuit of Literacy*, Michael Sampson (Ed.), Kendall/Hunt, Dubuque, Iowa.

Newman, J. (1988) 'Online: Logo and the Language Arts' in *Language Arts 65*, 6 (October) pp. 598–605.

Pengelly, H. (1986) 'Learning to write mathematics by writing mathematics'. Paper presented at the National BLIPS Mathematics Conference, Canberra, October 1986, mimeograph.

Pengelly, H. (1988) 'Towards a Mathematical Way of Thinking' in *Intercom 19.10.88* S.A. Catholic Education, Adelaide.

Piaget, J. (1973) *To Understand is to Invent*, Grossman, New York.

Skemp, R. (1977) 'Relational Understanding and Instrumental Understanding' in *Mathematics Teaching, No. 77*, Dec.

Smith, F. (1988) *Joining the Literacy Club: Further essays into education.* Portsmouth, NH: Heinemann.

von Glaserfeld, E. (1983) 'Learning as a Constructive Activity' in Bergeron, J.C. & Herscovics (Eds) *PME-NA North American Chapter of the International Group for the Psychology of Mathematics, Proceedings of the Fifth Annual Meeting, Montreal Sept 29–Oct 1.*

2

Acquiring the language of mathematics

Helen Pengelly

Pengelly focusses the basis of the discussion on what we're actually meaning when we use mathematics in conjunction with language. She investigates the influence the language curriculum is having on mathematics programs and offers principles for putting these into practice. Pengelly is critical of recent trends in which language principles are applied at a surface level resulting in children presenting a trivialised response to mathematical experiences. Her examples from children's work indicate a classroom where teachers have a clear understanding of mathematics and the learning process needed to plan a responsive, evolving curriculum.

The mathematics connection

A great deal of interest and literature is being generated about the mathematics-language connection. There are several ways these two words have been linked, including:
- mathematics and language
- the language of mathematics
- mathematics as a language
- mathematical language
- language and mathematics
- mathematical terminology
- acquiring the language of mathematics
- language and learning mathematics
- links between the language and mathematics curriculums
- the language of teaching mathematics
- the language in student's mathematical text.

   When discussing the mathematics-language topic, is the perspective always made clear? What is meant when 'mathematics' and 'language' are used in conjunction with one another? Despite generating quite distinct meanings, these terms appear to be used interchangeably, in non-specific ways, as global statements referring to any or all of the above. Meaning is rarely made explicit and has to be inferred and deciphered through reference to context. A more focussed and meaningful discussion is possible if the terms are defined and the particular interpretation outlined.

This paper begins by discussing the influence language curriculum is having on mathematics programs. The second part then describes some of the principles of language learning in practice in mathematics classrooms. Examples from eight-, nine- and ten-year-old children are used to describe the construction of fraction knowledge to illustrate these principles in action.

PART ONE: THEORETICAL ESSENTIALS

Curriculum context

Successful innovation in the language curriculum

The nature of language curriculum has changed markedly in the past two decades. The concept of what language is and how it is learnt is now considered in a much more wholistic way. Learning to read, for example, now starts with literature, its meaning and its purpose, and environments are planned which give children experiences from which skills and concepts about language and print can gradually be acquired and developed. No longer is language defined by sequenced, skill-based content. Neither does it advocate the repetitive, drill-and-practice exercises of text and stencil material. Language has moved away from believing these types of materials are useful resources.

This is because language curriculum has reconceptualised what language is and how it is best learnt and taught. While these developments have changed the way language is taught, mathematics has kept a much more conventional perspective. The emergence of so many new text series in mathematics, which do not differ significantly from conventional series, is an indication of this. Can the wealth of information about language curriculum assist in the transformation of the mathematics curriculum?

Problems of innovation in the maths curriculum

While problem solving, using materials, language and mathematics, girls and mathematics, real life applications, modelling and technology are issues in mathematics today, they have not managed to redefine teachers' perceptions of what mathematics is. In teacher support materials these issues are not incorporated into the fabric of a restructured curriculum. Instead they appear as adjuncts to existing curriculum. To primary school teachers, mathematics is a prescribed pre-determined way of thinking. Deviating from this path is difficult because it leads them away from the understandings they have about the nature and function of mathematics. With a lack of confidence in their own mathematics and in the absence of quality resources, it is difficult for teachers to venture beyond conventional methods. In the final analysis, teachers feel they are under pressure to develop basic competencies – and do not see how ad hoc problem-solving activities, for example, can achieve their curriculum objectives. New trends do not sit comfortably with old expectations and many questions remain unresolved. How are the skills and knowledge required for problem-solving learnt? How do problem-solving activities assist students in developing skills and making generalisations about broader mathematical principles?

Curriculum materials have also failed to describe a mathematics program which allows children to actively construct their own mathematics. Conventional methods still dominate mathematics teaching, although they are being scrutinised by teachers. As confidence and competence in new methods of teaching language grows, teachers are increasingly aware of conflict between the ideologies underpinning their language and mathematics curriculums. The way mathematics has been taught is no longer consistent with beliefs about learning. Consequently some teachers are reviewing the mathematics curriculum in the light of what they now know about teaching and learning: and in striving to find links in philosophy and practice, the strategies for language teaching are being employed in mathematics lessons. There are now many instances where the characteristics of language learning are common practice in mathematics classrooms. But in transferring the practices from one curriculum area to another there are pitfalls to be avoided.

Important differences between the mathematics and language disciplines

How can the principles of good language learning be employed in mathematics curriculum? 'Big Books', for example, are used in language as a means of sharing a story and modelling print to groups of children. Publishers are also producing an extensive variety of mathematics 'Big Books'. The assumption is that if children learn to read by reading then they will also learn mathematics by reading. I do not believe such an easily drawn conclusion is valid.

The purpose of 'Big Books' is to simultaneously give a number of children access to print. Modelling print is a vital component of any reading and writing curriculum, just as models of mathematical ideas, processes and structures are crucial to mathematics learning. They give children access to knowledge, skills and processes. But activities with manipulative materials, selected to model aspects of mathematics, are more likely than print to provide a learning environment where children can actively construct their own mathematics. 'Success in mathematics is a block away, not a book away,' as one student teacher said.

Using print to model mathematics is a secondary, non-manipulative experience. Research evidence suggests that young children learn mathematics best when thinking develops out of personal and active experiences with manipulative mathematical models. In the beginning, it is the materials themselves that capture the attention of a child. But, by continually engaging with these models, thoughts about mathematics begin to take shape. Gradually, the materials become the vehicle for thinking rather than an end in themselves. In the same way children gain satisfaction from re-reading a favourite book, children are motivated to continually revisit mathematical ideas. From this ongoing process, mathematical thinking becomes more sophisticated and complex as ideas are generalised and abstracted. Increasingly symbolic representations evolve as expressions of these ideas.

For this to occur, mathematical experiences need to model more significant mathematics than the current, specific-behavioural-objectives means of describing content allows. The processes involved in acquiring mathematics are as important as content. Mathematics is not a static body of knowledge, but knowledge actively built up by each learner as a result of his or her actions and interactions. Success in mathematics involves being able to think mathematically in new and unfamiliar situations. The processes of abstracting, generalising, symbolising, proving and solving, along with the many process skills (including classification and pattern) have to be established along with content as fundamental descriptions of mathematics.

The place of writing

Writing is another feature of the language curriculum which is becoming incorporated into mathematics lessons. The catchcry 'children learn to write by writing' has been interpreted into the mathematics classroom to mean children will learn mathematics by writing. Consequently, children are asked to write about the mathematics they do.

How often are children expected to write about something they have just written? And the trend in mathematics classrooms influenced by language principles has been to get children to write about their mathematical experiences. This creates trivial responses, many of which have been illustrated in published articles and in papers presented at conferences. *'I did maths today and it was fun'*, or, *'In maths today we did polydrons. I like polydrons'*, or, *'I did maths with Sally today. I like doing maths with Sally'*, or, *'Number 12 is the most fantastic number. I would say the number 12 is the best number in the whole wide world'*.

If children are to learn to write mathematics, they need experiences writing mathematics. This is a distinctly different form of writing to the writing children do in language lessons. Finding ways *to record and communicate mathematical ideas and processes* encourages development in mathematical thinking. Writing mathematics, rather than writing about what was done in a lesson, will result in quite a different outcome. To make a distinction between these different forms of writing, children are asked to *record* their mathematics rather than to write it. This seems to keep options open by not limiting responses to prose. When first coming into contact with new mathematical ideas or materials it is common for a child to be pre-occupied by them. This is reflected in recordings as children use words to describe the experience or pictures depicting the actual physical involvement. As experiences become familiar and the mathematical ideas gain prominence, the representations cease attending to context, indicating that the thoughts are now directed towards the mathematical ideas and relationships. These representations gradually take on the context free, precise, concise and symbolic characteristics of mathematical language. Contextual information is deemed extraneous and irrelevant to the mathematical investigation. Children learn to write mathematics by writing *mathematics*.

The dangers of mistaken inferencing in curriculum development

In using the knowledge gained about language learning to develop the mathematics curriculum, we have fallen into the trap of transferring the practices of language teaching to the mathematics classroom – mathematics 'Big Books', journals, writing, class sharing and so on. With such a superficial interpretation of the links between these two curriculums, it is likely that the rigour of mathematical reasoning will be lost in all the language processes that surround it. When looking at how language knowledge can assist in the restructuring of the mathematics curriculum, we need to understand the reasons behind changes in language learning and use these underlying principles as guidelines for curriculum development in mathematics.

Mathematics if not about writing journals, reading books or describing what was done in a mathematics session. Mathematical learning comes about as a result of engaging in the mathematising process. I am not suggesting the advance in our knowledge of language learning and teaching is not useful to mathematics, it is, but we must look at the principles underlying practice, and find ways to incorporate them into the mathematics curriculum in a way which suits the nature of mathematics. Cambourne's conditions for learning are as appropriate to the mathematics classroom as they are to a language class. Immersion, demonstration, feedback, approximation, expectation of teacher, responsibility, practice and feedback are also features of good mathematics teaching, but will exhibit themselves in different ways.

Towards a meaningful maths curriculum

If children are to learn meaningful mathematics, then it is not enough to immerse them in an environment filled with equipment and having teachers respond to whatever might arise out of random activity. The environment has to be carefully planned, structured and resourced. Mathematics lessons, like good language programs, require thoughtful preparation and selective resourcing. Each lesson has to be planned within the framework of the overall mathematics curriculum. Coherence and continuity eventuate when long term purposes and expectations are established. Teaching is then able to respond to prior learning, to provide appropriate experiences to support the existing learning, and at the same time establish the framework and the challenge for the learning that is still to come. To do this, activities have to encompass a comprehensive view of mathematics.

By interacting with models of mathematics which incorporate mathematical structures and relationships as well as specific ideas and skills, children have access to a mathematics beyond that normally found in schools. No longer are activities which demonstrate skills and concepts enough – they must also provide opportunities for relational and structural meaning to develop, each lesson taking long term goals into account while at the same time acknowledging short term outcomes.

Having a sense of destination will create the framework in which a teacher can understand current learning from a more comprehensive mathematical perspective. No longer will activities without long term purpose suffice. Activities must do more than demonstrate a concept or procedure. They should embody a chunk of mathematics in a way which enables the learner, by using the materials again and again, to construct an ever-expanding view of the mathematics being modelled. Activities need to be evaluated by their ability to generate mathematical thinking. The skills and concepts gained during this process provide demonstrable outcomes that monitor the growth towards greater understandings. Although skills are learnt within a broader mathematical context, there are similarities which resemble objectives in scope and sequence statements. The traditional expectations of naming and computing are not negated, but seen in a wider setting. Arithmetic, for example, is to mathematics as spelling is to language. Both are important, but only as tools. With this wholistic approach, learning continually strives towards its goals, while acknowledging the processes and understandings required to teach them.

PART TWO: PRACTICAL EXAMPLES

Learning the language of mathematics

This section uses examples from children's files to analyse development in thinking and the use of language to explore the concept of fractions.

Access to idea via experience

Before it is possible to talk or write about a mathematical idea, a child has to have begun to think abut it. Therefore, initiation into any novel field of mathematical learning is through experiences with mathematical models. In the sample used for this paper, children used a variety of

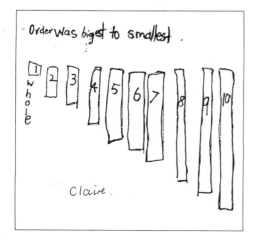

Fig. 1

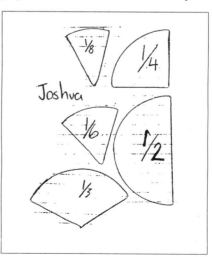

Fig. 2

fraction kits to value and order pieces in any one set when the largest block was assigned the value of one (Figures 1 and 2).

All children were given their own sets of material. They were also grouped with other children doing a similar task. This enabled them to 'do their own thing', while at the same time always having access to other people's thoughts. Sharing ideas and talking issues through were valued. Very little recording was expected during this initial stage. Once children were comfortable naming and ordering the pieces in several sets, they were challenged to find how many different ways they could use the pieces within a set to make up the value of one. In order to keep track of the combinations they found it useful to keep records (Figures 3, 4 and 5).

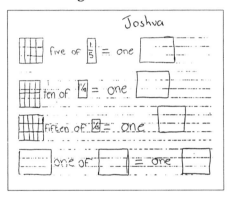

Fig. 3

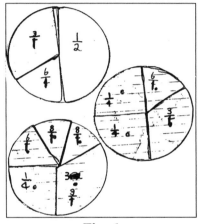

Fig. 4

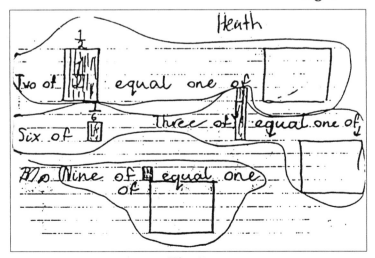

Fig. 5

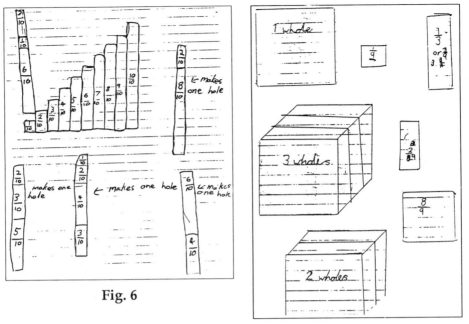

Fig. 6

Fig. 7

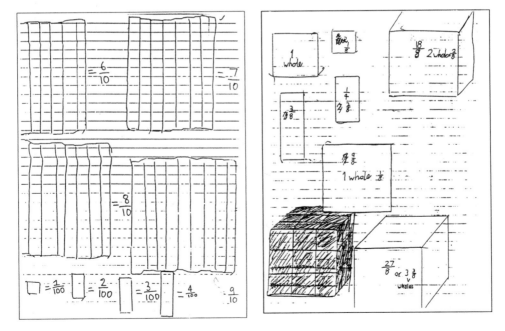

Fig. 8

Fig. 9

Rather than seeing the exercise as one of merely labelling, different blocks within a set were assigned the value of one. This encouraged children to focus on the relationships between blocks, keeping the activity open and maintaining interest in the exploration for several weeks (Figures 6, 7, 8, and 9), along with other mathematical studies.

Developing the idea

By actively engaging in mathematical investigations and reflecting on these experiences, mathematical understandings form and grow. During this phase children also explore ways of representing the ideas they are generating. Along with their thinking, the style, form and focus of their recordings developed markedly throughout this phase. Physical models remained important as the thought processes still depended on the stimulus of physical activity. Once a basic understanding of fractions had been established, the challenge to 'find as many ways as possible to make one' continued to capture the children's attention. As they were also investigating base ten, it was opportune to introduce decimal fractions. Cuisenaire rods and base ten blocks were used as models. In the first instance, the 'ten' rod was assigned as one. Later, the 'hundred' block was valued at one. At this stage of their learning about fractions all children were asked to record their findings (Figures 10 and 11).

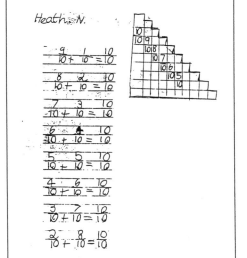

Fig. 10

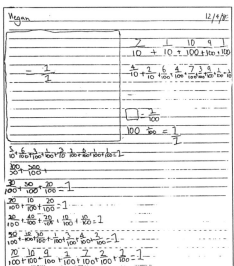

Fig. 11

Throughout these investigations, the balance in children's recording changed from predominantly words, pictures and diagrams to mathematical symbols. Physical models were giving way to mental images, although new challenges usually required assistance from manipulative models.

Whatever an individual did or recorded was accepted as an expression of what made sense at that particular phase in learning. Teachers responded by using this knowledge, together with an understanding of mathematics and the learning process to plan a responsive, evolving curriculum.

The next challenge for this group of children arose when they discovered different numbers could describe the same fraction. Once again, a seemingly simple task of, 'How many different ways can you find to describe the same fraction?' (Figures 12-27), generated interest that lasted for weeks (other mathematical topics were investigated concurrently).

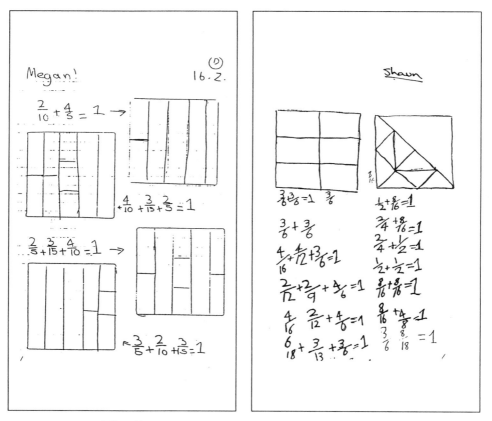

Fig. 12   Fig. 13

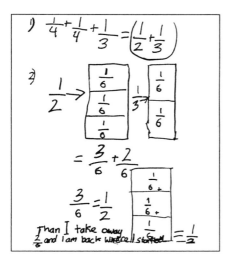

Fig. 14

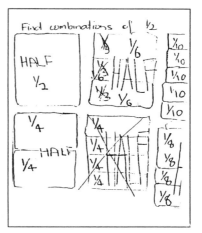

Fig. 15

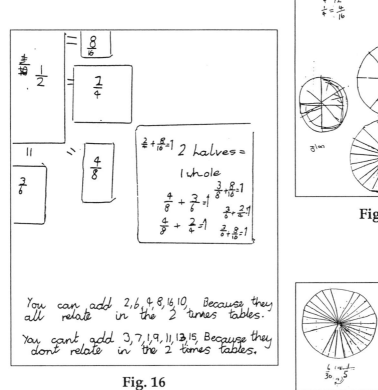

Fig. 16

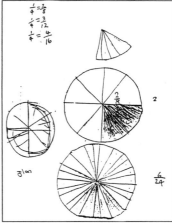

Fig. 17

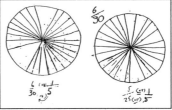

Fig. 18

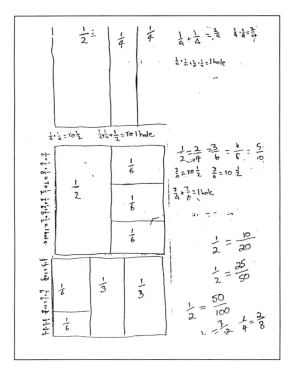

Fig. 19

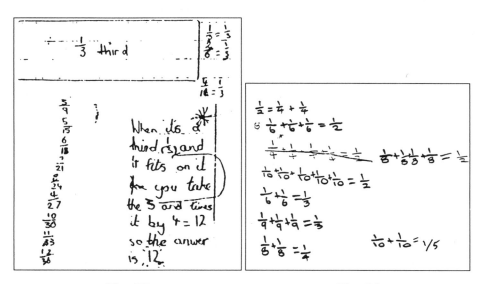

Fig. 20   Fig. 21

Playing with mathematical ideas and developing rules

By this stage it was not the physical activity maintaining the interest of students, it was the ideas themselves and an innate desire to establish relationships and identify rules. Materials were less important. A system of symbols had evolved from their investigation and was used instead of materials to meaningfully manipulate the ideas. Although the materials were still available, children relied on them less and less. They worked with ideas by operating with symbols, relying on the mental images built out of experience. While it is obviously much more efficient to think with pen and paper, unless the ideas have been abstracted from personal experience and the symbols seen as viable descriptions of it, then manipulation of symbols will rely on rote recall of rules and procedures.

Heath's calculations (Figures 22–25) are his response to, 'What other fractions can you find equivalent to one-half, one-third...? Megan's many sheets of workings, summarised efficiently in Figure 26, utilise her knowledge of tables and number patterns.

The amount of self initiated repetition and practice is evident in all of these examples (Figures 22–27). Abstracting, symbolising and generalising mathematical principles were emerging out of this investigation. This level of thinking was made possible by the continuing opportunities to address the ideas.

$\left(\frac{1}{2}\right)$		$\left(\frac{1}{3}\right)$	
$\frac{2}{4}$	$2\div2=1$, $2\div4=2$	$\frac{3}{9}$	$3\div3=1$, $3\div9=3$
$\frac{3}{6}$	$3\div3=1$, $3\div6=2$	$\frac{4}{12}$	$4\div4=1$, $4\div12=3$
$\frac{4}{8}$	$4\div4=1$, $4\div8=2$	$\frac{5}{15}$	$5\div5=1$, $5\div15=3$
$\frac{5}{10}$	$5\div5=1$, $5\div10=2$	$\frac{6}{18}$	$6\div6=1$, $6\div18=3$
$\frac{6}{12}$	$6\div6=1$, $6\div12=2$	$\frac{7}{21}$	$7\div7=1$, $7\div21=3$
$\frac{7}{14}$	$7\div7=1$, $7\div14=2$	$\frac{8}{24}$	$8\div8=1$, $8\div24=3$
$\frac{8}{16}$	$8\div8=1$, $8\div16=2$	$\frac{9}{27}$	$9\div9=1$, $9\div27=3$
$\frac{9}{18}$	$9\div9=1$, $9\div18=2$	$\frac{10}{30}$	$10\div10=1$, $10\div30=3$
$\frac{10}{20}$	$10\div10=1$, $10\div20=2$	$\frac{11}{33}$	$11\div11=1$, $11\div33=3$
$\frac{11}{22}$	$11\div11=1$, $11\div22=2$	$\frac{12}{36}$	$12\div12=1$, $12\div36=3$

Fig. 22

$\left(\frac{1}{4}\right)$		$\left(\frac{1}{5}\right)$	
$\frac{4}{16}$	$4\div4=1$, $4\div16=4$	$\frac{5}{25}$	$5\div5=1$, $5\div25=5$
$\frac{5}{20}$	$5\div5=1$, $5\div20=4$	$\frac{6}{30}$	$6\div6=1$, $6\div30=5$
$\frac{6}{24}$	$6\div6=1$, $6\div24=4$	$\frac{7}{35}$	$7\div7=1$, $7\div35=5$
$\frac{7}{28}$	$7\div7=1$, $7\div28=4$	$\frac{8}{40}$	$8\div8=1$, $8\div40=5$
$\frac{8}{31}$	$8\div8=1$, $8\div31=4$	$\frac{9}{45}$	$9\div9=1$, $9\div45=5$
$\frac{9}{35}$	$9\div9=1$, $9\div35=4$	$\frac{10}{50}$	$10\div10=1$, $10\div50=5$
$\frac{10}{39}$	$10\div10=1$, $10\div39=4$	$\frac{11}{55}$	$11\div11=1$, $11\div55=5$
$\frac{11}{43}$	$11\div11=1$, $11\div43=4$	$\frac{12}{60}$	$12\div12=1$, $12\div60=5$
$\frac{12}{47}$	$12\div12=1$, $12\div47=4$	$\frac{13}{65}$	$13\div13=1$, $13\div65=5$
$\frac{13}{51}$	$13\div13=1$, $13\div51=4$	$\frac{14}{70}$	$14\div14=1$, $14\div70=5$

Fig. 23

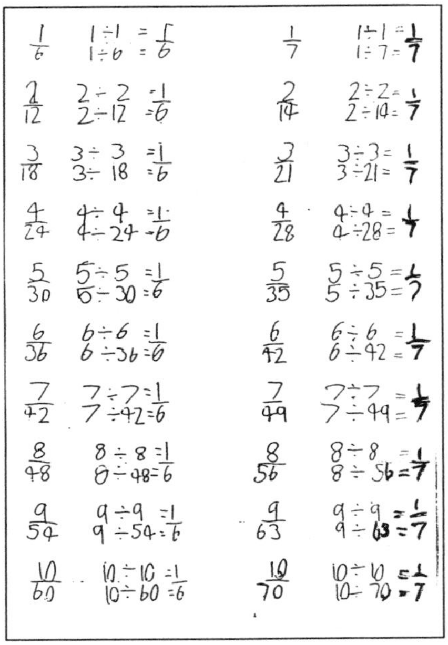

Fig. 24

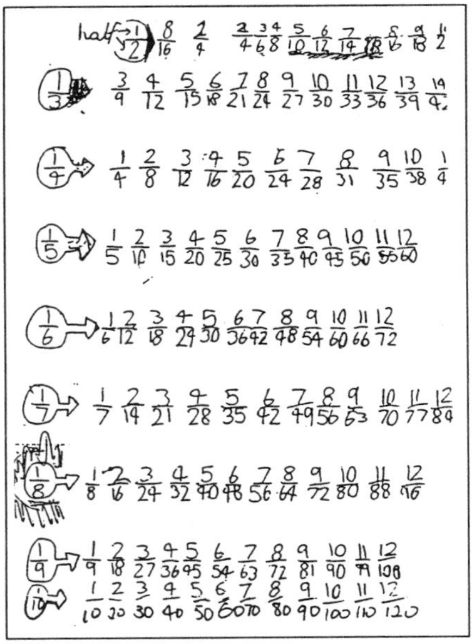

Fig. 25

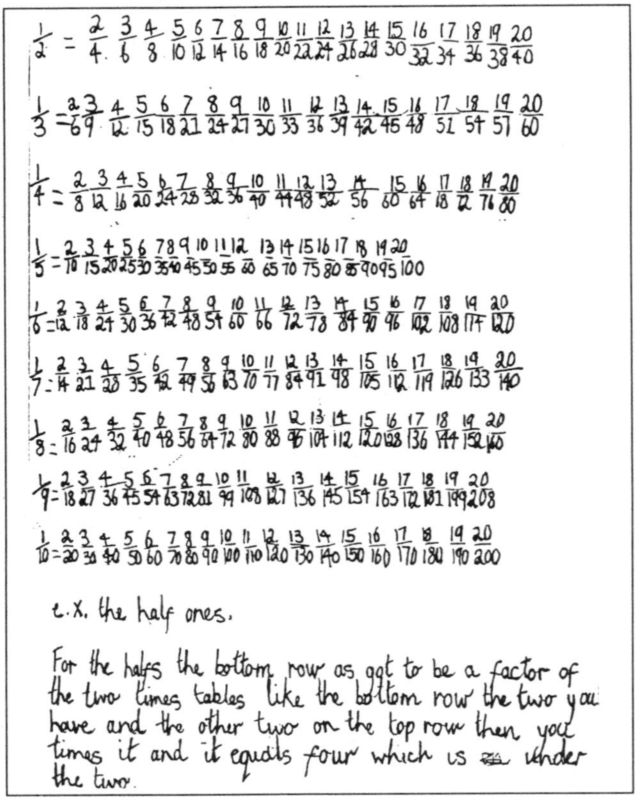

e.x. the half ones.

For the halfs the bottom row as got to be a factor of
the two times tables like the bottom row the two you
have and the other two on the top row then you
times it and it equals four which is ~~z~~ under
the two.

Fig. 26

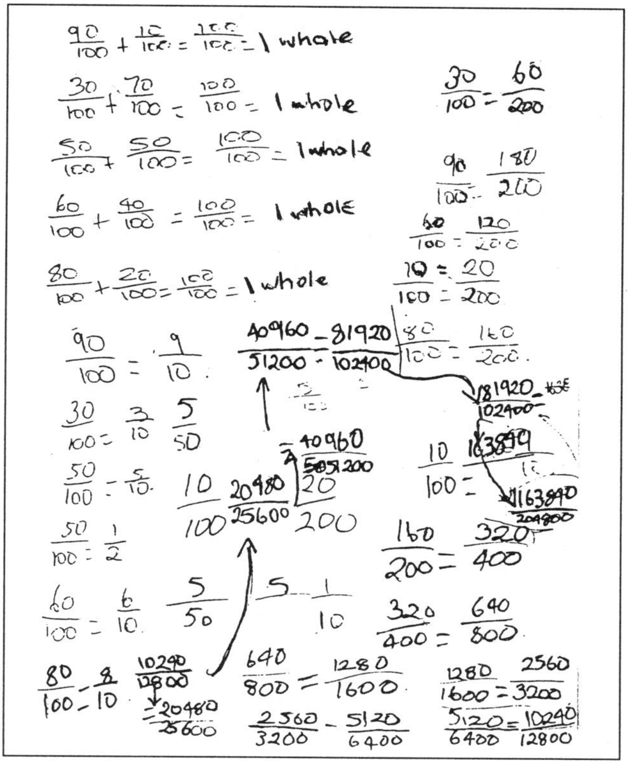

Fig. 27

Louise's recording (Figure 27) indicates her delight, intrigue and independence when exploring equivalent fractions. The skills she developed were an outcome of the investigation, not the focus of it. Computation was valued as a means to an end, not an end in itself. Having expressed hundredths as tenths:

$$\frac{90}{100} = \frac{9}{10}, \ \dots \ \frac{80}{100} = \frac{8}{10},$$ she decided to deviate from the

original task to explore other ways of describing $\frac{8}{10}$

She generated the following fractions

$$\frac{80}{100} = \frac{160}{200}, \ \frac{160}{200} = \frac{320}{400}, \ \frac{320}{400} = \frac{640}{800}$$

$$\dots \ \frac{10\,240}{12\,800} = \frac{20\,480}{25\,600}, \ \dots \ \frac{81\,920}{102\,400} = \frac{163\,840}{204\,800}$$

as all equivalent to $\frac{8}{10}$.

Of course, the investigation did not stop here. 'What is the rule when you are dealing with fractions where the numerator is not one?' (Figure 28) is just one of the avenues these children continued to explore. The mathematising process continued.

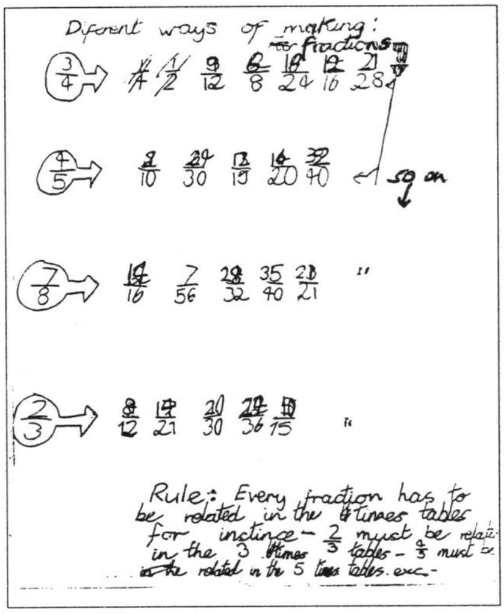

Fig. 28

Conclusion

The strategies for language learning do not transfer directly into mathematics teaching. These strategies have been selected and developed because they create a classroom environment which reflects principles of learning. Mathematics teaching can also employ the principles of ownership, challenge and individuality. These strategies need to be conducive to the development of mathematics.

3

An emerging model of
the language of mathematics

Sue Gawned

Gawned attempts to grapple with a framework or model that suggests current perceptions about language learning can be integrated with mathematical learning. The motivation sprung from the need to organise data being collected from classrooms in which teachers were trying to implement language-learning principles into mathematics. The framework recognises that the language that children come to school already knowing has its roots in 'real world' language from social interaction. Children from pre-school on become part of a process where the language demands of the classroom bring change. The language becomes activity specific and gets expressed in the construction of meaning of mathematical concepts and processes.

The Carawatha Language Development Centre trialled this model and their article is included in this issue.

During the introduction to a recent workshop on the new Western Australian Mathematics Curriculum, one of the presenters enthusiastically announced: *There is currently a revolution in mathematics'* and then explained how some of the changes in the new curriculum reflected this 'revolution'. While many would agree with the presenter, others would say they've been teaching mathematics this way successfully for years. However, one aspect that has come to the fore quite recently is the interest in the role of language in mathematics instruction and learning. This development may reflect the increasing emphasis on the evaluation of teaching style and focus in the mathematics stream, but it is also an inevitable consequence of the large volume of research into literacy acquisition and the evaluation of language and literacy learning in our schools.

In 1988 and 1989 the Commonwealth Schools Commission funded the Curtin University of Technology's Language of Mathematics Project Team as a Project of National Significance.

The Western Australian Early Childhood Education Mathematics and Language Project was conceived to develop and trial approaches to early childhood mathematics education that evolved from principles of a naturalistic, oral and written language learning theory. One of our aims for the project was to examine aspects of the existing early childhood mathematics curricula (K-3) to identify underlying language requirements for mathematics learning and instruction. A second aim was to identify the language needs related to aspects of problem-solving in mathematics at this level (K-3).

One of the questions that faced our project team from the outset concerned constructing or finding a model of the language of mathematics.

Why provide a model?

A model can provide a guiding framework.

At a micro-level of focus it serves to:
• structure observations
• facilitate the organisation of the data
• assist in implementation of any implications arising from the findings.

At a macro-level, a model often contributes to:
• the identification of what's missing in our knowledge or data base
• the evaluation of new studies
• the explanation of problems or questions

Requirements of the model

To achieve these aims, such a model needed to be:
• sufficiently broad to encompass the area under study
• sufficiently explicit to apply to one aspect of the whole or to explain the findings of a focussed study in the context of the whole.

Obviously we needed a model to investigate those aspects of the language of mathematics which most interested us, but we were also interested in explaining our findings in terms to suit research generally. Further, we wanted a model that would help us answer some of the questions which teachers were presenting to us, such as:

1 What language do children require and use for mathematics?

2 How important is language to success in mathematics? Which components are important at particular stages of development?

3 How different is the language of mathematics from the language of other curricula, such as literacy, science, or philosophy?

4 What aspects of the language of mathematics are difficult for children? What variation exists?

5 What is the role of 'scaffolding' in mathematics instruction?

As our project team was working primarily with early childhood teachers, who were participating in the action research component of the project, our specific goal was to address the needs of these teachers. They wanted a model that would explain the role language played for them in their instruction of mathematics, and for their students in learning mathematics. They wanted a model that was clear and easy to apply to the real world of their classroom.

During the early part of the study, the process of model building occupied a large part of our team's discussions. One of our criteria for the proposed model was that it relate to our theoretical position on language-learning generally.

The socio-psycho-linguistic model

The socio-psycho-linguistic model has been defined by a number of leading researchers, notably Wells (1984) and Wood (1988). This three-component model recognises the two-way process involved in a child's language learning:

1 that of the child, seeking to communicate with others in her environment and, motivated to this end, learning the language required by the multiple communication context she experiences;

2 that of the adult, facilitating the development of communication by adapting the demands of the situation to the child's capabilities, and extending the child's participation in the exchange.

At any time in a communication context, the three components will be represented in some way. They may be defined as follows:

• *The social component* of the model acknowledges that language develops from and through social interaction and is used to achieve social purposes. Children quickly learn those forms of language which are needed for social purposes.

• *The psychological (or cognitive) component* of the model acknowledges that the child is an active processor of language and information. Learning is a complex task of constantly receiving incoming infor-

LANGUAGE IN MATHEMATICS: THE SOCIO-PSYCHO-LINGUISTIC MODEL

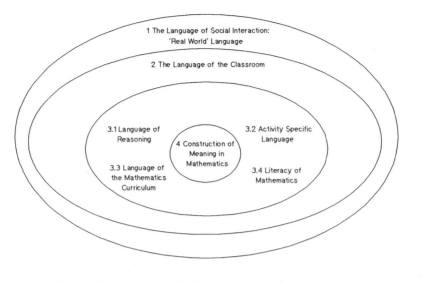

Fig 1: The proposed circular model

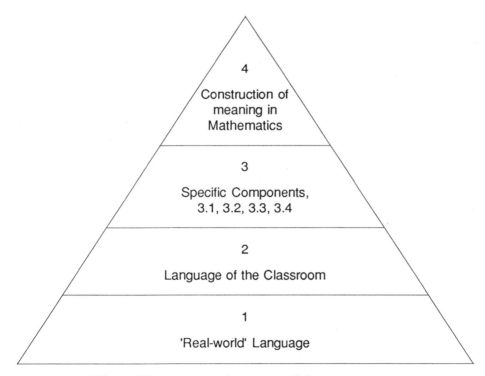

Fig. 2: The proposed cone model

mation, checking to see how it fits and then making adjustments to these new understandings.

• *The linguistic component* acknowledges that the child has to learn the standard forms and uses of the mother tongue (Zubrick and Shortland-Jones, 1988).

In applying this model of language learning to the construction of a model of the language of mathematics, we wanted to begin at the beginning: where the foundations of mathematics and also the foundations of the language of learning are being developed. Figures 1 and 2 and, later, Figure 5, are intended to be different perspectives of a 3-dimensional representation of the socio-psycho-linguistic model as it is applied to mathematics. The diagrams attempt to capture the interdependence of each component to the total construct we have of mathematical concepts.

The origins of the language of mathematics are rooted in the child's first experiences in the world. The way people communicate with young children, especially the language they use, aids the organisation of the child's own perceptions and concrete experiences.

Level 1: The language of social interaction

Language helps give shape to these internal (mental) and external experiences. They are given names and descriptions. Their use begins to fit into predictable patterns. Children develop scheme for daily or other regular events on to which new language is then mapped.

Simultaneously, the child's own perceptions and experiences serve as a stimulus for him to initiate interaction and to communicate with those around him. Thus, the language of social interaction is a construction that evolves from and in both directions. This is represented graphically in Figure 3.

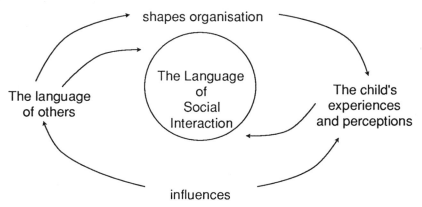

Fig. 3: The formation of the language of social interaction

The language of social interaction is the foundation for all subsequent language development and is one of the means of transmitting the social conventions of the culture. Children only acquire certain, necessary, non-verbal communication skills while interacting with others:

• turntaking
• negotiating turns
• understanding indirect and non-verbal messages
• maintaining the topic of discussion
• introducing new topics with sufficient information for the listener.

These skills are important in shaping the child's ability to negotiate meaning with others.

It is via interaction at home, in play with peers, in the pre-school, that the language of the culture derives meaning. Thus it became the foundation circle for our model, or the bottom of the cone (if viewed as a 3-dimensional model).

Within this first component of the model, many children are also laying the foundations for a number of specific components depicted higher up or further along in the composite model. These are:

• the language of reasoning
• the language of the mathematics curriculum
• activity-specific language
• the literacy of mathematics

1.1 The language of reasoning

We know that children use language that reflects the decision-making that occurs in their play. This is the beginning of the language of reasoning or problem-solving. Children verbally plan scenarios and actions, organise things and each other, monitor each others' behaviour and comment on the success of their achievements (evaluation). They select, compare, reflect, make predictions, infer, justify (until the cows come home!), re-count and re-enact events over and over. They also generalise what they have learned to new situations.

1.2 Language of the mathematics curriculum

We know that children are also intrinsically fascinated by order, sequences, and pattern (including number), and that in play either alone or with siblings, peers or adults, are often exploring aspects of the mathematics curriculum long before they reach school. If some of these explorations do occur with adults, or able older siblings, it is likely that the basis of some of the language of the early mathematics curriculum is also quite familiar to them prior to school entry – for example, shape, size, concept names, terms used for measurement of space and quantity, and certainly number terms.

1.3 Activity specific language/syntax

Similarly, children often hear different language genres modelled during the day to day interactions in the home. For example *procedural genre* may be used when a parent is re-defining the going-to-bed routine or re-stating the consequences of certain behaviour. On a more positive note, it is the genre that will also be used when describing how to make pancakes or playdough. *Descriptive genre* may predominate when children discuss plans for their birthday parties and describe the birthday cakes of their choice. Much *explanatory language* is modelled in the course of family life and many children come to school well-versed in this genre when applied to social behaviour and consequences. Thus activity specific language also has its foundations in the 'real-world' language the child experiences prior to school.

1.4 Literacy of mathematics

While not all children will have opportunities to develop rudimentary mathematical literacy skills prior to school, children generally are surrounded by mathematical literacy conventions in our environment. For example, numbers are much in evidence in shops, on roads, cars, houses, clocks, money, television and video machines. Attention to these literary uses occurs informally again in these interactions with the 'real world'.

Level 2: The language of the classroom

None of the above four components occurs next in sequence in our model. Rather, we chose to singularly set the language of the classroom as the second major level of development in the overall schema.

While the pre-school year and its well integrated 'hands on' curricula facilitate the transition from home to school, moving from the pre-school to the more formal world of the primary classroom is recognised as a demanding transition for many children. We wanted the model to capture some of what was happening for children at this time, in respect to the particular language demands this transition brings.

Research over the past decade has shown that the classroom has a particular 'language' of its own. It is quite different from discourse relationships the child experiences at home or at play, even in a wider social context. Classroom discourse is characterised by:
• being highly rule-bound
• operating within a fairly tightly defined set of relationships

• being instruction-dominated.

There is almost always an expert adult who functions variously as facilitator, instructor, carer or controller. This adult relates primarily to a large groups of novices but also to smaller groups and individuals.

Research by Green and Smith (1983) and Duchan (1989) has shown that classroom activities display two levels of discourse. If we consider a mathematics activity, the first level (or 'frame') will be one that focusses the students on the mathematics component. This may include such elements as:

• presentation of the materials or problem
• task instructions, possibly including an example or model
• expectations regarding the outcome
• clarifying questions to check the students' understanding.

Parallel to this 'content and process' frame, which in our example is the mathematics frame, is a co-occurring frame which guides participation rules or requirements. Students need to be attuned to this organisational structure and to the discourse rules that apply within the structure. While having to listen and comprehend the primarily verbal information within Frame 1, they frequently have to *infer* the rules of participation since there are generally given implicitly or non-verbally. Students have to understand and internalise the appropriate set of organisational principles for any one classroom in which they participate. These principles will include rules or procedures about such things as:

• receiving group instruction and not generally requiring individual direction
• ways of requesting assistance (while the teacher is engaged elsewhere) that do not disrupt the lesson flow.

For young children to focus successfully on the primary discourse frame, i.e. the mathematics 'frame', they first need to understand the language of the classroom: they need to know and use the classroom discourse rules for listening and participation; for learning and co-operating in a group; for negotiating assistance. Children who adapt well to the different organisational structures of the classroom, those who demonstrate an understanding of classroom communication rules, have been shown to be more successful students as they progress through school (Green and Smith, 1983).

Level 3: Specific language of mathematics components

At the next level of the model, four components of the language of mathematics have been differentiated. We propose that these components develop in relation to each other, hence the intersecting circles, although they may not develop at the same pace or time.

Together with the former 2 levels, they contribute to building more specific mathematical meaning for the student. Again the components identified are:

• the language of reasoning (or problem solving)
• the language of the mathematics curriculum
• activity specific language
• the literacy of mathematics.

3.1 Language of reasoning (or problem solving language)

While the language that accompanies and supports specific math-based activities tends to reflect specific aspects of the activity, there is nothing particularly mathematical about it. The language of reasoning refers to the language used by both teachers and children in mathematics-based problem solving contexts:

1 the language the teacher models to encourage the child's use of one or other problem solving process or strategy;
2 the language the child uses while exploring the problem at a cognitive, metacognitive or metalinguistic level.

There are several schools of thought in the current debate on the role of problem solving in mathematics in Australian schools, two examples being the process approach and the metacognitive approach. However, regardless of the preferred approach, or alternatively whether an eclectic approach is used, the language of the problem solving task needs to be considered: the core language required by the student to solve mathematics in an interactive, problem solving setting is going to be the same.

There are many examples of problem solving language. Specific types of language reflect associated or underlying steps in the problem solving process (not necessarily hierarchical), as presented in Figure 4.

Thus, different steps in problem solving reveal a different predominance of 'reasoning' type of language, or different combinations of 'problem solving' language. However, most of the language registers of problem solving have two features in common. We know that:

1 Complex sentences are the most efficient means of expressing these abstract or more complex ideas. (Complex sentences are those with two main verbs.)
2 Co-ordinating or subordinating conjunctions *because, so, if...then,* are the primary means of accurately expressing the complex meaning relationships in statements such as inferences, justifications, comparison and predictions.

There is some evidence that the language of reasoning develops out of the language of reflection and only after the language of description and comparison is well established (Gawned, 1989). The language of reflection refers to the language used to describe one's own thinking/ reasoning processes, for example: in the planning stage, a young student might talk aloud as follows:

I might use these 2 soft forms to build a big triangle with equal sides. Oh, I think it'll work better with 3! Let me see, I'll need to use the same size triangles. I wonder if these are the same size. Yes– that's it.

Eventually, this sort of language becomes an internal sort of chatter but it still serves the same purpose. Reflective language is a part of the language we use when thinking, either aloud or mentally. It is a more complex form of language because it involves joining ideas together, making explanations and justifications. Causal relationships are central to reasoning. For example: a student is explaining how he made a graph:

I put these numbers from 1 up to 10 along the side because that's how many things I measured. And I put these numbers 10 up to 100 along this side because 10 was the smallest thing and 100 was the longest thing in my collection.

There is groundswell evidence that where the language of reasoning and reflection is used explicitly by the classroom teacher, students are empowered to use this same language – indeed, the same processes – in their problem solving. A number of researchers suggest that students who have mastery over the language they use for reasoning and explaining outcomes are those who use more appropriate strategies in mathematical problem solving (Wood, 1988). Thus, the language of reasoning becomes an important area for monitoring in mathematics. We need to ask:

• Do students have sufficient opportunity to hear such language being used to aid problem solving?
• Are students appropriately encouraged when they demonstrate reflective, reasoned approaches to problem solving?
• How much of this sort of language is demanded in problem solving tasks set for students?

The role of the adult as scaffolder becomes important when considering this aspect of the language of mathematics (Bickmore-Brand and Gawned, 1989; this volume).

Some of the steps in problem solving		The language corresponding to each step
Planning	→ ←	*Procedural language:* the sequencing of intentions demands understanding of relationships of order/time.
Reflection on the issues	→ ←	*Descriptive language:* to clarify the various components involved. *Reflective language,* e.g. use of reflective nouns (*idea, thought*), and verbs (*think, wonder, imagine, mean, know*) to describe the reflective process.
Reasoning about various aspects of the task	→ ←	The *language of reasoning* itself is varied. It may include comparison, prediction, inference, consideration, e.g. use of the verbs and adverbs of possibility (*might, maybe, if…then suppose*).
Explanation e.g. evaluation of stage reached	→ ←	The *language of explanation* may include: • description plus justification
summary of outcome	→ ←	• recounting, pulling threads together
generalisation of conclusion	→ ←	• prediction plus justification.
Monitoring and evaluation of the learning process	→ ←	Explanatory language: description and summary, including *prediction* of what might happen next time.

Fig. 4: Components of problem solving language

3.2 The language of the mathematics curriculum

The language of the mathematics curriculum is the language, often symbolic, which is specific to mathematics. The meaning of this language can only be learned in the context of mathematics. The process begins when the child learns a new word in the context of a mathematics activity or realises that a word or phrase that has carried a particular meaning until now has a rather different and specific meaning in mathematics. Conversely, words may acquire more relative status in these new contexts. Terms such as 'take away', 'equals', 'goes into second place', have to be considered in a new light in formal mathematics. For example: differentiation of the term 'multiply', which in conversational or literary contexts means grow in number, in a mathematics context will usually refer to the specific mathematical operation. Examples are numerous, and the issues well addressed in the relevant literature.

The language of the mathematics curriculum needs to be learned in order for children to succeed in mathematics. Such learning includes an acceptance of ambiguity of word meanings. Most students are able to embrace the notion of specific meanings in a specific context, but it poses problems for some. As mathematics curricula are being reviewed and re-written, there seems to be increasing attention being given to this component of the language of mathematics. It belongs primarily in the teacher's arena: it is the teacher's awareness of possible ambiguity of word meaning or difficulty with unfamiliar terms that will serve to clarify the mathematical meaning intended.

Of course, students will need sufficient opportunities to develop and use the language of the mathematics curriculum in order to develop understanding of what such specific terms and language mean. This is perhaps the most 'transparent' component of the whole model.

3.3. Activity-specific language

Mathematics tasks and activities take many diverse forms in today's classrooms. It is becoming increasingly important to identify the language demands of particular tasks and how these vary from activity to activity.

Different activities will demand language from one or two predominant language genres. *This may not be 'mathematical' language but a type of language that functions as the medium for the mathematics to be learned.* In the classroom context, for example, a classification activity may draw on *descriptive* language more than any other genre. It is useful to ask whether the young students have the descriptive language they need to participate successfully in the activity. For example, do they have the requisite labels, attribute terms, noun phrase constructions, to express the relationships they're observing? Alternatively, it could be that *procedural language* is required if students were asked to explain how and why they classified a group of items as they did. To do this they have to use language in a more sequential way, enumerating the steps they followed, explaining and justifying the outcome.

Identifying the language of the mathematics curriculum (3.2) is certainly a primary goal. However, it is not sufficient to inform us of the language demands of mathematics activities within any one strand of the mathematics curriculum. A knowledge of language genre and of the particular language demands in mathematics activities is important in monitoring student performance.

3.4 The literacy of mathematics

Representation and recording are central aspects of school-based mathematics, of building mathematical literacy. In the child's first years of developing the written language of mathematics, broad-based concepts are important as well as new and specific symbolic forms and their meanings. The child first learns ways to represent what is familiar. Each then learns to use these mathematical representations to record maths events, such as by using symbolic language, diagrams and numerals. As children become math-literate, they have:

1 greater understanding of how best to represent operations and processes used and the outcomes obtained.

2 greater access to the creation of mathematics problems and events.

The representation and recording of mathematics is becoming more diverse as the activity base of mathematics widens. For example, young children are involved in graph building, diagramming and mapping, whereas once the major literacy focus for these children would have been learning to write digits accurately. Functional, 'real-world' mathematics is reflected in this component of the language of mathematics. Young children need to understand that the various forms of representation they learn to use will make up 'the language of mathematics'. This will make mathematical literacy even more meaningful.

One area of literacy applied to mathematics we need to pay particular attention to concerns syntax: the sentence structures used for written mathematical problems. The sentence complexity of written instructions and problems needs to be monitored and matched to the students' level of language comprehension. The language complexity demanded in the students' written responses to such problems also needs to be monitored: do the students have the written language skills necessary to give adequate and accurate accounts of their solutions? The written language skills of the student become a key factor when considering success in mathematics through the primary years. Research is growing in this area, and should continue to inform us of the relevant issues (MacGregor, 1989).

Level 4: Construction of meaning in mathematics

This model functions as a flat circular model with all components intersecting or contributing to the students' success in mathematics at any one time. The model is also intended to be developmental in a constructive sense. It attempts to identify the origins of the language of mathematics and where this development moves to. Hopefully, this is the point where mathematics is meaningful for the student as well as the teacher.

The model can also be represented along a continuum or series of continua, although the interactive nature of the components is not easy to depict in a linear model. Thus, if Figure 2, the proposed cone model, is turned on its side, it more clearly represents a continuum of development (Figure 5).

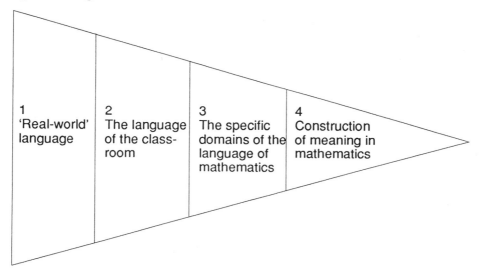

Fig. 5: The language of mathematics continuum

Conclusion

This model represents our current understanding of the way language functions at different levels and in various domains to make a significant contribution to:

• the child's understanding of mathematics in the classroom
• their successful participation in classroom mathematics
• the continual building of new knowledge and understanding in mathematics through the primary years.

In today's classrooms, the language of social interaction or 'real-world' language is an acknowledged part of classroom participation. It is often the medium for a child's expression of self-esteem, and of confidence as a member of his or her social group. It is important to be competent with social language, given the current style of classroom organisation and emphasis on group learning in mathematics.

The rules of classroom communication are a constant that need to be learned or spelled out if modified. They are crucial to a child's success in school generally, but in mathematics in particular, with the emphasis on verbal instruction and problem solving.

As we have suggested, the other four areas defined by the model contribute in varying degrees in any single mathematics activity. No mathematic activity is devoid of language.

Mathematical literacy, while a developing area through the school years, first emerges in some of the rudimentary systems of recording that children themselves discover in their pre-school years. The value of recording outcomes at a pre-numerate or early stage of numeracy acquisition is now well established (Pengelly, 1989).

In answer to our initial question 'Do we have an emerging model of the language of mathematics?' this multi-level model emerged from our project work. It has been applied by a number of schools to their mathematics programs, to answer the questions:

1 How well do we understand the role of language in mathematics programming, instruction and evaluation?
2 How well are we incorporating this understanding in our mathematics programming, instruction and evaluation?

The accompanying article in this issue by a team at the Carawatha Language Development Centre takes up the model at this point (with minor modifications), to look at its application to a current classroom mathematics program.

The model is intended as an initial framework in which to examine the major language components contributing to mathematics instruction and the student's construction of meaning in mathematics.

References

Duchan, J. (1989) 'Evaluating adults' talk to children: assessing adult attunement', *Seminars in Speech and Language, 10*, 1.

Gawned, S. (1989) 'The language of classification', *Australian Journal of Reading, 12*, 2.

Gawned, S. (1989) 'The role of language in mathematics and a new look at scaffolding', Paper presented at the National Association of Speech and Hearing Conference, Perth, April 1989.

Green, J. & Smith, D. (1983) 'Teaching and learning: A linguistic perspective', *The Elementary School Journal, 83,* 4.

MacGregor, M. (1989) 'Reading and writing mathematics', *Australian Journal of Reading, 12,* 2.

Pengelly, H. (1989) 'Mapping mathematical meaning through writing', *Australian Journal of Reading, 12 ,* 2.

Wells, G. (1981) *Learning through interaction: The study of language development.* New York: Cambridge University Press.

Wood, D. (1988) *How children think and learn..* Cambridge, MA: Blackwell.

Zubrick, A. & Shortland-Jones, B. (1988) 'A socio-psycholinguistic view of language and language learning', *The Language In-Service Course (LINC),* Curtin University of Technology and Ministry of Education, Perth, WA.

4

Scaffolding for improved

mathematical understanding

Jennie Bickmore-Brand and Sue Gawned

Bickmore-Brand and Gawned look at the different interpretations of scaffolding from the Vygotsky to Graves perspectives. The current debate comes down to a question of roles and responsibilities for the adult-child interaction. Scaffolding has its roots in modelling, and the potential development of metacognitive strategies makes its application for mathematics particularly important. For scaffolding to be effective, it must be jointly constructed between mentor and learner, and will enhance the learner if it has a self-destruct nature. The latter part of the paper provides results of research by Gawned into scaffolding being used with mathematical concept development. The study indicates the roles teachers and children need to take on board if scaffolding is to be a comfortable classroom practice. The paper closes with a transcript of scaffolding in action.

This paper begins by giving an historical perspective on the practice of 'scaffolding' as dealt with by researchers in the field of language development. It then discusses the findings of an extensive study conducted in Western Australian primary schools where scaffolding practices were actively used by adults to assist pupils in their mathematical problem-solving. The paper offers implications for the class environment, the teacher's role, the child's role and for curriculum activities/ materials.

What is 'scaffolding'?
Scaffolding is the practice of building on what the child appears to know in order to stretch the child to the next stage of development.

Some of the key features of scaffolding which emerged from my research into this area form the basis of the discussion:

• the roles and responsibilities of the adult and child in scaffolding
• the joint construction of meaning between adult and child
• the capacity of scaffolding to enhance the learner's potential
• the self-destructive nature of the supporting language of scaffolding.

Scaffolding – the debate

No discussion on scaffolding can ignore the current debate across Australia concerning its interpretation. At this point I will briefly outline the issue for debate as it relates to my interpretation of scaffolding. (Gray, 1987, offers a balanced look at both sides of the argument.)

If we accept that most teaching involves instruction then some debate can focus on the timing of the point of instruction and the overtness with which it is done. Even from within the natural language learning camp this debate is being heard; that is, the argument comes from within the advocates of constructivism rather than their traditional opponents, the reductionists.

Who then are the chief players? On one side there are the followers of Cambourne (1988) who, within his natural language learning conditions relies upon 'demonstration' as the only real instructional tool. Cambourne (1988) has, of late, included scaffolding as a significant component in both his 'Use' and 'Response' conditions for learning.

However, Cambourne (1988) like Graves (1983), Holdaway (1986) and others sitting comfortably with his conditions of learning, would see the child's responsibility for extracting the instructional potential from a situation as having greater sway in the learning process than any direct instruction on the part of the teacher/parent. Their interaction with the child, they maintain, is not directive and is not controlled by the adult/teacher.

The other point of view, being held by other natural language learning exponents such as Vygotsky (1962), Bruner (1978), Cazden (1983), Ninio and Bruner (1978), and Halliday (1975) is that in the learning context the dyad of 'mentor' and 'learner' provides the instructional opportunity which enhances the learning process. Here the adult/teacher takes on a specific instructional role, quite unashamedly. It is interesting to note that Lehr (1985) saw the work of Graves (1983) as being consistent with Bruner's (1978) notions of scaffolding.

Fundamentally the debate comes down to a question of roles and responsibilities for learning. I would argue that the more Graves and his like are investigated and actually observed in operation with children, the greater their function as informed guide, channelling the paths that children take, becomes obvious, and can be seen as having a directed scaffolding role.

While scaffolding has its roots in modelling, it also has ramifications for the metacognitive strategies that children use. The language the adults use in the scaffolding context acts as a good resource for a child's own reflection and operations.

If scaffolding is to have a place in mathematics instruction it will assist teachers who are currently unsure whether the discovery approach to learning is correct or the traditional didactic approach should be sustained. Most teachers today find this dilemma very real; they do not feel comfortable about leaving children to deduce the strategies and mathematical concepts for themselves, neither do they wish to resort to teaching concepts and strategies by direct instruction followed by sustained practice by the children. Scaffolding, I believe, utilises components from each.

Scaffolding – interpretations and situations

Vygotsky (1962) is recognised as the founder of the label of 'scaffolding' for the specific interactions which occur between adult/expert and child/learner. His research observed how children's intellectual and linguistic development arose out of their interaction with the significant adults in their lives. He saw these adults as having an important function which assisted the children to reach their potential development, which he believed would not be reached under age or maturation alone.

Vygotsky termed this the *'zone of proximal development'*, where instruction leads the child to focus on aspects of learning (such as speaking, reading and/or writing) in a joint problem-solving context which eventually will be independently handled by the child.

Ninio and Bruner (1978) have been the most influential in their advocacy of scaffolding. Their famous example shows a study of a dyad of a mother with a young infant, where a ritual occurred in the dialogue rather than in pure imitation; although the mother would operate with imitation, at times, of the child's gestures and noises. In spite of the one-sided nature of the language abilities the two are seen jointly constructing meaning: the scaffolding is in pace with the child and in the context of satisfying interaction.

The child finds out by the responses of adults what he is assumed to mean by what he is saying.

(Holzman, 1972, p. 312)

This dialogue cycle of turn taking is also in line with research by Stern (1975) and Snow (1976).

Similarly Chall and Snow (1982) see the interactional times with significant adults as enriching the child's cognitive storehouse for school literacy tasks. Children who have had the benefits of these forms of interactions do considerably better in the early years of school. (See also Tizzard 1985)

Lehr (1985) recaps Bruner's (1978) concept of scaffolding as being a temporary framework providing a platform for the next step towards more 'adult' communication. An example of this is provided by mothers who try to prevent their children from slipping back, at the same time demanding more complex performances. Thus Lehr (1985) has focussed on the developmental aspect of scaffolding, which may be regarded as one of the most significant, from an educational perspective. This is also in line with the self-destruct nature of scaffolding to be discussed later.

Roles and responsibilities of adult and child

One of the challenging aspects of scaffolding is what effect it has on roles and responsibilities. Searle (1984) raises the issue of who is in control of the language when teachers take on scaffolding as a teaching strategy. There needs to be a flexibility of roles. At times the role will be traditional with the child being the learner and the adult being the teacher and at others the child will take on the lead and use the teacher's language while the adult is more passive and non-directive.

Searle (1984) refers to Bruner and Ratner (1978) who identify some features which contribute to effective scaffolding including 'a familiar semantic domain, predictable structures, role reversibility, variability, and playfulness' (Searle p. 480).

Lehr (1985) also identifies two forms of scaffolding in Cazden's (1983) work: (a) *vertical constructions* and (b) *game-like routines.*

(a) *vertical constructions* were also described by Scollon's (1976) work who, like Bruner (1983), saw the adult extending language progressively. Scollon (1976) noted that after time the child began to take over both roles, i.e.: of teacher and learner, and he felt that this would be an advantage for the discourse processes involved in classroom reading and writing.

(b) *game-like routines* include peek-a-boo games and picture book reading, and other predictable pattern conversations between mother and child. The adult initially takes on both roles of the dialogue, being speaker/instructor and responder/learner, accepting gross approximations of 'language' from the child. Gradually the adult relinquishes her role of child as the child's ability to sustain the dialogue improves. Ultimately the child begins to reverse role with the mother and initiates much of the interaction, directing the mother or playing both parts solely by herself.

Wells (1981), in his observations of scaffolding practices during his research on language development (quoted in Lehr, 1985), also notes this feature of turn taking and the instructional role the adult takes on during a dialogue. The child internalises the adult language and is in a position to direct herself using the same cues.

The growing degree of control that occurs when children take over their own actions in supportive contexts is another function that emerges from the use of scaffolding (McKenzie 1985). This is the notion of responsibility which Cambourne (1988) and Graves (1983) both wish for their learners. The 'scaffolders' recognise that it cannot exist as total responsibility from the outset. If children are given the opportunity they will develop this responsibility, provided they are challenged and allowed to take risks.

The focus is on the intention of the message on the part of the learner/student, Both Bruner (1983) and Graves (1983) would agree that, in regard to the focus for scaffolding, the adult works to support the child in achieving an intended outcome. The adult is aware of the level of development of the child and *'follows the contours of child growth'* (Graves 1983, p. 271).

The role-reversal also influences the metacognitive processing of scaffolding; the child gradually internalises the procedures for thinking. Tizzard (1984) noted that there was a reciprocal process between the adult and the child. Young children between the ages of 3 and 5 who were seen to ask the most searching questions were the ones whose parents were most likely to answer them fully and, of course, the parents who were most likely to answer were the ones with children most likely to ask. The children's questions exhibited a high incidence of similarity to the adult's language patterns (see also Halliday 1975). Cambourne (1988) looks at the change in role as the 'expert' gradually withdraws. Consequently as the classroom routines become established the boundaries blur between the roles of 'expert' and 'learner', at times reversing and inevitably shifting with each interaction.

Adult and child: joint construction of meaning

Cairney (1987) looks at the tailoring by the adult of his dialogue to ensure a shared construction of meaning. He quotes Snow (1983) who looked at pre-schoolers and parental interaction being facilitated in three ways:

1 Adults will often continue and extend the topic that the child intro-
duces – *semantic contingency*.

2 Adults will use a predictable structure to the dialogue in order to
allow for more complex interactions and to reduce the uncertainty –
scaffolding.

3 Adults will be aware of what the child can do and will insist on
certain levels of performance – *accountability*.

The interactional nature of language growth was also stressed by
Halliday (1981) who referred to it as 'two way', explaining that inter-
action provides a contextual resource within the significant people of
children's lives and enables transfer into less familiar communications.
This is a true test for the viability of knowledge according to von
Glaserfeld (1983).

The capacity of scaffolding to enhance the learner's potential

Regardless of the 'when' of scaffolding, the strength of the scaffolding
debate as I see it is embodied in the words of Gray (1987) when he
wrote about children constructing *'meanings which they would have been
unable to achieve if left to their own devices'* (p. 9).

Cambourne (1988) is also concerned with helping the learner to reach
his/her full potential and notes that interaction with an adult usually
serves to extend or modify the learner's control of what he/she is
trying to learn. Cambourne refers to it as *'raising the ante'* which occurs
*'when parents and others refuse to let the learner/talker regress to an earlier,
less conventional form of expression'* (p. 78). The adult is not necessarily
providing the answer, but challenges the learner to make the deductions.

This form of adult feedback refers to that moment when someone
who knows more about, for example, the written form of the language
than the learner does, engages with the learner's approximation and
lets him/her know either that it is acceptable or that it is not conventional
and that some modifications are necessary. Cambourne (1988) fleshes
out what he sees as the most common interactions in scaffolding:

• focussing – on a gap which the learner needs
• extending – challenging or raising the ante
• refocussing – encouraging clarification
• redirecting – offering new information if there is a mismatch between the learner's intent and the message or in the teacher's expectations of the capacity of the learner (p. 117).

Cross (1978) documented scaffolding with attention to the adult's speech, which projected action and developed the child rather than simply reiterated what is or what was. The main purpose behind getting the learner to grow and stretch with the questioning and response of the 'expert' is that they will eventually internalise them and ultimately ask these questions of themselves.

Vygotsky (1962) argued that *'the most effective learning occurs when the adult draws the child out to the jointly constructed "potential" level of performance'* (in Gray, p. 11). It is the support of the adult who knows the 'appropriate' cultural context for the language and the child, which allows the child to develop his potential in his own rate and without any loss of ownership. *'It is the loan of consciousness that gets the child through the zone of proximal development'*, (Bruner 1986, p. 132 emphasis added).

The self-destruct nature of scaffolding

A natural consequence of scaffolding which enhances the learner's potential is that it is developmental and therefore as the child gains mastery the scaffolding is taken away or no longer used – it self-destructs (Cazden, 1983, p. 10).

As children take over the control of the language they go through a stage of imitating the scaffolding language the adult has used. Staton (1984) evidenced scaffolding in kindergarten where children after initial modelling by the teacher were able to extend their own dialogue and take on the role of the teacher in prompting and self questioning. This degree of control extended to where the child took *'over the question asking and direct(s) the teacher to help her when she needs it'* (Staton, 1984, in Lehr, 1985, p. 669). Meanwhile the teacher has constructed new scaffolding to replace the previous point for the child.

Classroom research using scaffolding as a strategy for problem-solving

The following study was written up by Gawned (1989) and presented in detail in the *Australian Journal of Reading* (Focus Issue on Language and Mathematics) Volume 12 Number 2 June 1989.

The task and procedure: 20 kindergarten and 20 Year 3 children from seven Western Australian primary schools participated in the study. Individually each child was invited to play a classification (sorting) game. Kindergarten children were requested to sort 20 animal objects into three groups and Year 3 children used 20 animal pictures. Once the items were sorted into three groups, a fourth container was presented and the children asked to make a fourth group.

The adults were directed to explain the task, modelling actions if necessary, and then to facilitate each child's exploration of the materials and the task using verbal scaffolding to assist each child towards a resolution.

An observational checklist which provided additional data on how the children completed the task was combined with data from the audiotape transcripts of each adult–child interaction. Questions designed to elicit verbal justification, for example, 'Why do these animals go together?' were addressed to each child as they derived a grouping, in order to facilitate children's language for reasoning as they engaged in the task.

While the study discusses in detail the language capacities (content, form and use) of pupils as they performed the task, a continuum was developed which summarised the relationship between the children's ability to perform the task and their language capacity (see Figure 1).

Figure 1: The relationship between the children's abilities and their discourse

LESS ABLE LANGUAGE USERS	CHILDREN USING SELF-DIRECTIVE LANGUAGE	ABLE LANGUAGE USERS
Poor classification skills.	Emerging classification skills.	Ability to resolve classification task.
Children required scaffolding to begin task, unable to resolve the task.	Scaffolding assisted children's abilities to explore the task and derive a solution.	Resolution reached without scaffolding. Justification readily

The **Less Able Language Users** consisted of kindergarten children with poor language ability, in terms of comprehension and expression, and poor discourse skills, who demonstrated little or no classification skills on this task. The scaffolding, however, enabled them to attempt the task and arbitrarily sort the objects.

The **Children Using Self-Directive Language** consisted of an even mix of kindergarten and Year 3 children who interacted comfortably with the adult or used self-directed, task-directed language, i.e. they were able to use a wider range of meanings, forms and functions when they used language. These children set up a 'dialogue' with themselves, by making a comment or question and then answering themselves. The scaffolding assisted them to explore the notion of classification beyond just labelling and to resolve the task.

The **Able Language Users** consisted of Year 3 children who were capable communicators of their ideas, who were able to explain what they had done to complete the task and the majority of whom were able to offer an alternative solution. These children needed no scaffolding and perceived their role in the discourse to respond to any adult requests for explanation/justification.

Scaffolding styles

What also emerged from the research were three types of scaffolding techniques:

• Task focussed
• Child focussed
• Multi-focussed

Task focussed style

This style tended to adhere to the formal requirements of the task.

Question use
• A minimum number of questions overall
• Served a formal rather than a facilitatory purpose
• Content-oriented questions
• A–B/A–B/A–B/ sequence, (A = Adult; B = Child).

Response Style
• Brief, unexpanded
• Affirm or negate rather than comment
• Serve to maintain the child on task

Child focussed style

Supports the child in which ever way they choose to explore the task.

Question use
• High proportion of general questions
• Few follow-up or specific questions
• Often directed to the child's feelings or wishes.

Response style
• Supportive, encourages content
• Non-differentiating, i.e. positive whether the child had made a sound or an incorrect/inappropriate one.
• Content reflects the children's content. Little new information offered.

Multi-focussed style

This provides scaffolding to meet the needs of the particular child at each point during the task when a shared focus is seen to be beneficial.

Question use
- Range of question types
- Question sequences interspersed by informative or directive comments, e.g. Aq– Aq– Ac– B/ Aq– Ac– B– Ac/ Ac– Bq– Ac/ Bq– Aq– Bc/. (A = Adult; B = Child; q = Question; c = Comment.)

Response style
- Varied according to child's needs.

Implications

The question that needs to be asked at this stage is how can the historical research findings about the scaffolding which succeeds in developing language together with this study of mathematical scaffolding of language and concept development be applied to the classroom context for mathematics?

Implications for the environment

Provide an interactive classroom context for mathematics!
- Encourage and model purposeful, exploratory, supportive classroom talk in mathematics events as in literacy events.
- Use the language of shared contexts, by labelling, describing and comparing.
- Reflect out aloud and justify your own actions as a teacher in a mathematical event.
- Encourage other adults, teachers, parents, visitors to participate in mathematical activities with the children.
- Provide real life tasks that are meaningful to the children and where mathematics is used as a means to an end.
- Allow the children to experience independence and control and to accept responsibility for their actions.
- Recognise that the whole class is a resource and that children can seek assistance from many sources.
- Avoid asking children to dwell on what they already know.
- Avoid single solutions to problems; i.e. avoid having specific answers in mind. Listen to the response with an open mind.
- Provide as many opportunities as you can for two to four children to work together.

- Watch that the more verbal children don't do all the talking. Match children in small groups with children of around the same verbal ability.
- Allow children the choice to be participant or observer.
- Encourage classroom exploratory language:
  'Why do you think...?'
  'How might...?'
  'What would happen in...?'
- Reverse the usual classroom discourse rules and roles.

Implications for the teacher's role

Be a major *participant* in mathematical activities, scaffold the child and the activity so that the child is extended
a) in mathematics, and
b) in developing the language to handle mathematics.
- Provide tasks that facilitate co-operation between the class members.
- Develop tasks which ensure genuine involvement and direct supervision when needed.
- Develop tasks which stimulate enquiry rather than have you provide a body of knowledge.
- Change your role to that of roving consultant rather than a director of learning.
- Make every child aware that you value his communication with you.
- Listen actively and not automatically.
- Model conversation 'repair' by asking clarifying questions when you don't understand fully, and encourage children to do the same.
- Extend the child's utterances for him/her.
- Recast the child's utterances in a more complex way.
- Use questions to focus on the salient aspects of the task.
- Use simplification questions when a child cannot respond. Lead him to the answer rather than failing him by moving on to another child.
- Use a variety of 'encouragers' when a child is stumbling verbally ('mmm', 'uh-uh', 'Truly?' 'I know'), or to encourage him to extend his length of turn.
- Leave a pause after your conversational turn, to encourage the child to respond.
- Encourage the development of reflective language by modelling:
  'Think...'
  'Do you remember...?'
  'Do you know...?'

'I wonder...'
'I guess...'
'I don't believe...'

Implications for the child's role

- Ensure the child has opportunities for interaction with:
  - ~ an adult participant
  - ~ a capable peer
  - ~ a group of peers and an adult participant.
- Ensure the child has opportunities to explore ideas, practise his/her new knowledge of mathematics and the new language of mathematics.
- Allow the child opportunities to develop the language for mathematics, e.g. the metacognitive abilities: labelling, description, comparison, reflective language, reasoning.
- Children should feel free to ask 'curiosity' questions.
- Children should seek opinions from a wide variety of sources.

Implications for the curriculum activities/materials

- Relate mathematical activities to background knowledge of the children.
- Use experiential and interactive activities.
- Relate mathematical activities to the child's interests.
- Ensure tasks are reasonably short to allow for achievement and practice.
- Include everyday contexts.
- Establish literature–mathematical links.
- Provide more open-ended activities where resolution of the task is required by a number of solutions.
- Use activities, materials/events where the child assumes increasing responsibility for the decision-making process.

Summary

In order to achieve effective scaffolding of mathematical activities the scaffolding must be tailored to the needs of the individual child. The scaffolding must be provided at any point during the task when a shared focus might be seen to be beneficial for the child. The adult scaffolding should consist of a blend of focus questions interspersed with comments, information, suggestions and modelling of metacognitive language and the language of the task

The following transcript analysis is provided to illustrate the process of scaffolding in the mathematical context of classification.

TASK: CLASSIFICATION OF ANIMAL PICTURES INTO THREE GROUPS

ADULT–CHILD DISCOURSE	SCAFFOLDING
A. *Why does the bird go in the group with no legs?*	*Request for explanation*
C. *Because birds don't have any legs. When they flying they don't have any legs 'cos they only use their wings.*	
A. *Oh, I see.*	
C. *I might have to change these ones (snake, flying birds, earthworm).*	
A. *Why do you think you might have to change them?*	*Request for explanation*
C. *Because they don't have any legs so they should really go with those ones here. (i.e. 'fish' group).* *These two are separate. (Bee and lady-bird).*	
A. *Can they fit into any of the groups?*	*Request for evaluation*
C. *No.*	
A. *Well, I wonder what we can do? We want to try to find a group for them. Let's think of a way to sort them into one of our three boxes.*	*Stating the joint goal*
C. *They can go into another group... Well what ones can be separate... because that one... the bee makes honey for you and the ladybird eats all the insects off the roses.*	
A. *So why would they go together?*	*Request for the comparative*
C. *Because they help you.*	
A. *Mm... that sounds like a good group. Can any of the other animals help you?*	*Acknowledgement* *Request for information*
C. *The fish can go there 'cos when you catch fish they make food for you.* *Put those there 'cos all of the animals with legs need their legs so they've got to go there.*	

A. But they've all got legs, haven't they?	Request for clarification
C. Put those there and those ones there.	
A. I wonder why you've put these ones together?	Request for explanation
C. Because they've all got four legs.	
A. And why did you put these ones together?	Request for explanation
C. Because they've got all sorts of legs. And then this one doesn't have any legs (includes all the birds).	
A. So you have the ones with four legs; then you have the ones with all sorts of legs; then you have the ones with no legs.	Summary statement (Review)

References

Bruner, J., (1983) 'Vygotsky: A historical and conceptual perspective' in *Culture, Communication and Cognition: Vygotskian perspectives*, (Ed.) James Hertsch, New York: Cambridge University Press; pp. 342-347.

Bruner, J., (1986) *Actual minds. Possible worlds*, Harvard University Press, Cambridge, Mass.

Bruner, J., and Ratner, N.(1978) 'Games, Social Exchange and The Acquisition of Language', *Journal of Child Language 5* ,I; pp. 391–401.

Cambourne, B., (1988)*The Whole Story: Natural Learning and the Acquisition of Literacy in the Classroom*, Ashton Scholastic, Gosford, New Zealand.

Cairney, T., (1987) 'The social foundations of literacy' in *Australian Journal of Reading*, 10, 2.

Cazden, C.B., (1983) 'Adult Assistance to Language Development: Scaffolds, Models, and Direct Instruction' in *Developing Literacy: Young Children's Use of Language*, R. Parker and F.A. Davis (Eds.) International Reading Association, Newark, D.E.

Chall, J., and Snow, C., (1982) *Families and Literacy: The Contribution of Out-of-School Experiences to Children's Acquisition of Literacy: Final Report*, Harvard University Graduate School of Education, Cambridge, Mass.

Cross, T.G., (1978) 'Mothers' Speech and its Association with Rate of Linguistic Development in Young Children' in *The Development of Communication*, N. Waterson and C.E. Snow (Eds.) Wiley, Chichester.

Gawned, S., (1989) 'The Language of Classification' in *Australian Journal of Reading*, 12, 2.

Graves, D., (1983) *Writing: Teachers and Children at Work* Portsmouth, NH: Heinemann.

Gray, B., (1987) 'How Natural is "Natural Language Teaching – Employing Wholistic Methodology in the Classroom"? in *Australian Journal of Early Childhood*, 12, 4.

Halliday, M.A.K. (1981) 'Three Aspects of Children's Language Development: Learning Language, Learning through Language, Learning about Language' in *Oral and Written Language Development Research: Impact on the Schools*, (Eds.) Yetta Goodman, Myna M. Haussler and Dorothy Strickland, Urbana Il, National Council of Teachers of English, Newark, Delaware, International Reading Association.

Holdaway, D., (1986) 'The Structure of Natural Learning as a Basis for Literacy Instruction' in *The Pursuit of Literacy*, M. Sampson (Ed.) Kendall/Hunt, Dubuque, Iowa.

Holzman, M., (1972) 'The use of interrogative forms in the verbal interaction of three mothers and their children' in *FPsycholing Res 1*, pp. 311–336.

Lehr, F., (1985) ERIC/RCS Report: 'Instructional Scaffolding' in *Language Arts*, 62.

McKenzie, M.G., (1985) 'Classroom Contexts for Language and Literacy' in *Observing the Language Learner*, A. Jagger and M. Trika (Eds.) International Reading Association: Urbana, IL: National Council of Teachers of English, Smith-Burke, Newark, D.E.(CS 208 718).

Ninio, A., & Bruner, J., (1978) 'The achievement and antecedents of labelling' in *Journal of Child Language* 5, pp. 1–15.

Searle, D., (1984) 'Scaffolding: Who's Building Whose Building?' in *Language Arts* 61.

Scollon, R., (1976) *Conversations with a one year old: A case study of the developmental foundation of syntax.* University Press, Honolulu, Hawaii.

Snow, C.E., (1976) 'The development of conversations between mothers and babies', *Pragmatics* microfiche 1.6.A2.

Staton, J., (1984) 'Thinking Together: Interaction in Children's Reasoning' in *Speaking and Writing K–12* , (Eds.) Christopher Thaiss and Charles Sihar, Urbana Il, National Council of Teachers of English.

Stern, D., (1975) 'The infant stimulus "world" during social interaction'. Paper presented at the Loch Lomond Symposium, University of Strathclyde.

Tizzard, B., & Hughes, M., (1985) *Young Children Learning*, Cambridge, MA: Harvard University Press.

von Glaserfeld, E. Steffe, L.P., Richards, J., & Cobb, P., (1983) *Children's counting types: Philosophy, theory, and application* Praeger, New York.

Vygotsky, L.S., (1962) *Thought and Language*, MIT Press, Cambridge, Mass.

Wells, G. (Ed.), (1981) *Learning Through Interaction: The Study of Language Development*, New York: Cambridge University Press.

5

The development of mathematical understanding

The Carawatha Language Development Centre

(M. Donovan, C. Blamey, E. George, M. Bishop, J. Crookham, A. Gyford, G. Manook, W. Strang, S. Leitaô)

The Carawatha Language Development Centre attempted to provide the practical links of the Gawned model (see article this issue), by implementing it into the classroom context. The teachers believed the transition from 'real world' mathematics to literate mathematics and its specific abstract language and concepts was not automatically achieved by many children. The teachers sought to use scaffolding to enable children to make a smooth transition between the two and to see the connections between the two.

The Carawatha Language Development Centre is a gazetted Special School which provides specialised language intervention on an intensive basis for children with normal non-verbal cognitive functioning, whose academic, emotional and social performance is severely limited by a profound neurological language delay/disorder.

As a major area of school development the staff of the Carawatha Language Development Centre decided to research current studies on the importance of the language of maths in the learning process and apply this in conjunction with our own existing knowledge of language to the maths curriculum.

Language development

Language development occurs along a continuum from the communicative, oral language of the home founded in the domain of concrete

operations to an increasingly more decontextualised literate, written language. According to Westby (1985), this development involves:
• function – why people talk
• topic – what people talk about; and
• structure – how people talk.

Many children, be they language delayed or mainstream, experience great difficulty in coping with the language of the classroom, particularly as it becomes more abstract (Blank 1978). Experiences must be provided to encourage a natural transition from oral language to functional literate language if the child is to achieve success at school. The authors believe that the Carawatha model provides a continuum on which children across the grades can be placed(see p. 65).

Mathematical development

When children are learning to talk they are confronted with language as a whole and this evolves along a continuum of developing complexity. It would seem logical to assume that children should also be allowed to gain a concept of mathematics as a whole and that mathematical learning should develop in a similar way.

The beginning of mathematical understanding commences at birth, and develops as children experience their world as a place of order, pattern and prediction. In these pre-school years, usually through the medium of play, the children become involved in activities such as labelling, sorting, classifying, sequencing, comparing, measuring and problem solving. Through these processes they will come to terms with the mathematical concepts of grouping, ordering and transforming.

As a result of this natural process of discovery, the foundations of mathematical learning are formed. Unfortunately this prior knowledge is often segmented into distinct, often unrelated units of mathematical learning when the child begins formal education; and the total concept of mathematics, particularly the language of maths, as being a functional part of everyday life is destroyed.

The Carawatha model

In an endeavour to avoid this splintered approach, and to ensure that there is a cohesive and functional policy to match the curriculum expectations across all grades, the staff developed a model based on a continuum of mathematical language development.

Objectives of the Carawatha model

- To establish a continuation of the development of understanding that occurs through all stages of learning.
- To define the importance of recognising the teaching of the language of mathematics in the learning process.
- To assist teachers entering the Centre to recognise the significance of the language of mathematics.
- To form a continual reminder that mathematical concepts and language should develop from exploration and experience at all grade levels and then progress to symbolic representation.
- To ensure that children commence new mathematical learning at a position along the continuum that matches their knowledge and ability rather than at a position designated by chronological age and curriculum expectations.
- To provide a framework for evaluation that:
  - ~ is appropriate to all grades
  - ~ avoids over emphasis on being right or wrong
  - ~ encourages discovery and initiative
  - ~ provides positive feedback
  - ~ allows the transfer of information and the sharing of ideas between all staff members.

The application of this model should ensure that the language of mathematics and the learning/teaching strategies used at the classroom level are inter-related and at the same time determine whether, as a school, staff are addressing the language of mathematics in day to day teaching.

Development of the Carawatha model

Although in its early stages of application, a number of important points are emerging from the model as staff focus on the four critical elements that provide meaning in maths, i.e. Problem Solving Language, Activity Specific Language, Language of the Maths Curriculum and Literacy in Mathematics (Gawned 1990, this issue).

- Maths and the language of mathematics is an integral part of all teaching and learning.
- There is not an automatic transition from real world maths to literate maths with its specific abstract language and concepts.
- Teachers need to provide the scaffolding to enable the child to make a smooth transition and see the connections between the two.
- Concrete experience and exploration is essential in the upper grades

THE CARAWATHA MODEL
The Language of Mathematics

THE LANGUAGE OF MATHEMATICS

Real World	Everyday language of Mathematics	Language of Maths Curriculum	Literacy in Mathematics
Activity Specific Language ←→	**Problem Solving Language** ←→	**Language of Maths Curriculum** ←→	**Literacy in Mathematics**

• Vocabulary
  e.g. Labels
  Location
• Attributes (Colour, shape, size)
• Function
• Description
  e.g. *Put in*
    stack
    take away
    collect
• Relationships
  e.g. *match*
    fit
    same as in/on
• Responding
	• Absorbing
	• Reasoning
	• Predicting
	• Exploring
	• Inferring
	• Comparing
	• Negating
	• Decision Making
	• Selecting
	• Justifying
	• Evaluating/True/False
	• Summarising
	• Clarifying
	• Generalising
		Set
		Subset
		Intersection
		Frames
		Diagrams
		Equality
		Language of: numeration
		  measurement
		  space
		  time
			Representations
			Using/Recordin in maths
			Symbolic Language
			Drawing
			Diagram
			Numerals
			Formulae

NON SPECIFIC TERMINOLOGY   SPECIFIC TERMINOLOGY

Note: For convenience sake this model has been placed along a continuum of developing mathematical understanding. It must be understood that these areas are continually interactive and their position on the continuum is not prescriptive but dependent upon intellectual capability, prior experience, knowledge required and the pre-determined outcomes of the process being taught.

in order for students to gain a true understanding and functional use of maths.

- There is a need to establish 'base lines' to avoid assumptions of prior knowledge or a lack of a known concept. Questions must be asked as to what the children already know, and which techniques can be used to determine their existing knowledge and informed decisions made in regard to what children need to learn.

- Evaluation techniques should be designed to measure the conceptual and language knowledge of the mathematical process being attempted. Often it is the child's inability to use the language of the task to explain a concept well understood that results in a teacher's belief that the child has failed to learn.

- Care should be taken that the fine and gross motor skills required for a task do not detract from the concept being taught. Children with difficulties in these areas may need to concentrate solely on the motor co-ordination required for some activities and in doing so fail to meet the specific demands of the lesson.

Application of the model

In order to provide practical links between the model and its classroom application, a series of activities will be presented to demonstrate how the language of mathematics can be developed along the continuum between the real world and maths literacy and create a learning environment that ensures that the teaching of maths is successful, meaningful and enjoyable.

MATH STRAND — NUMBER

Objective: Take a given number of objects from a set.

Focus: Real world → Language of maths curriculum.

Activity

Ingredients
- 9 eggs
- 7 piles of sultanas
- 4 cups of sugar
- 8 cups of flour
- 2 cups of milk

Activity Specific Language
We are going to make some biscuits.
Here are all the things we need.
(Show ingredients, name and discuss.)

Problem Solving Language

(Our recipe doesn't need all of these supplies.)

How many eggs are there? Count. (Answer: 9)

Eggs We need two eggs.

Take away two eggs. How many are left? (Answer: 7)

Flour How many cups of flour are there?

Guess without counting. (Answer: 8)

We need four cups of flour

Take away four cups of flour.

How many are left? (Answer: 4)

Follow a similar procedure for all ingredients.

Language of Math Curriculum

Ask the children to record what they did.

Recording

Recording procedures are not prescriptive but allow the children to record their own perceptions in their own way. Symbolic representation is optional.

We had 8 cups of flour.
We took away 4 cups of flour. There are 2 left.

P-2⊂7

Samples

Selecting the activity

- When selecting mathematical activities teachers must have a set focus and an established knowledge of the outcomes required.
- Instructions must be simple and specific to the task being set.
- Appropriate questions must be asked at the beginning of the activity to ensure that children understand what is required of them.
- Strategies to remind children of the task set should be incorporated into the activity.
- Children should be allowed to find their own conclusions where possible and not have an adult's pre-conceived outcome imposed upon them.
- Children should be encouraged to record their findings orally, pictorially, in written or symbolic form.

Introducing the activity

Children should be allowed to develop a knowledge of the structure of the game/activity. Initially the teacher will see the mathematical focus but the children will see the game to be played.

It is important that children have the opportunity to handle and examine the materials involved and have time to learn the rules of the game. When this knowledge is established the children will begin to focus on the mathematical concept and connected language for which the activity was initially planned (Pengelly, H. 1990).

Repeating the activity

Activities can be repeated or adapted to meet the demands of a new focus and outcome whilst still retaining the children's existing knowledge of the resources needed and the rules of the game.

Teachers have a tendency to use an activity once and then discard it. If it was successful use it again and again. How many times do we play Snakes and Ladders, Chinese Checkers, Noughts and Crosses, Monopoly® and card games with continued enjoyment and increasing skill?

Practical application

Objectives: Early time experience using tockers

Tockers provide experience in time measurement for younger children. They have a circular base and a triangular apex. When the apex of the triangle is placed down on a hard surface and released, the tocker rocks on its circular base. When the tocker stops rocking it has measured a small amount of time, usually 5, 10 or 15 seconds.

Focus: Real world → Literacy in Math

Activity Specific Language
• Superlatives and comparatives
• Discussion techniques
• Organisational language.

Problem Solving Language
1 Classifying duration
2 Organising role for group members
3 Working co-operatively.
4 Developing recording methods
5 Comparing and evaluating methods

Language of Math Curriculum
• Time terminology
• Cardinal number

Literacy in Math
• Developing recording techniques
• Evaluating efficiency of recording methods
• Cardinal numerals.

Activity 1
Children experiment with a selection of tockers, comparing the duration of movement. Tockers are classified into long, medium and short duration. Children organised themselves into small groups, each group taking one tocker of the same duration. Children find out and record how many hops, jumps and steps they can do in the time marked by the tocker.

Recording
Recording materials used may be concrete or graphic. On completion, children join the large group to share their findings and discuss their recording methods. Follow-up talk also considers reasons for differing results between groups.

Recording samples are kept in a file to show development throughout the year.

MATH STRAND — MEASUREMENT (2)

Objective: Early time and distance experience using tockers and trundle wheel.

Focus: Real world → Literacy in Math

Activity Specific Language
- Comparatives and superlatives
- Use of questions: 'How + long, far?'
- Organisational language
- Discussion techniques.

Problem Solving Language

1 Forming small, even groups
2 Devising a running order
3 Stopping and starting on signal
4 Measuring using a trundle
5 Working co-operatively
6 Developing recording methods.

Language of Math Curriculum
- Time terminology
- Length/distance terminology
- Cardinal and ordinal number.

Literacy in Math
- Use of recording methods
- Evaluation of efficiency recording methods
- Cardinal and ordinal numerals.

Activity 2

Short classroom activity uses a 5 second tocker to test how many actions can be done in the given time. Main activity takes place outside, preferably on the school oval. Children form themselves into small groups and devise a running order. Using the 5 second tocker, the teacher signals for each child to start and stop running in the given duration. Each child sits on the track at the place they stopped running. The distance that each child ran is then measured using a trundle wheel. This is organised so that each member has a turn at measuring distance for another class member.

Recording

The initial recording of distance is done on paper by each individual. On returning to the classroom, the small groups reform and work on recording the distance that all the group members ran. Graphic and concrete materials are available for use. Results and recording methods are shared with the whole group. Recording samples are kept in a file to show development throughout the year.

MATH STRAND — MEASUREMENT (3)

Objectives: Early time and length experience using stopwatch and trundle wheel.

Focus: Real World → Literacy in Math

Activity Specific Language

• Comparatives and superlatives
• Use of questions: 'How + long, far, quick fast...?'
• Organisational language
• Discussion techniques.

Problem Solving Language

Problem Solving:

1 Measuring distance using trundle wheel
2 Forming small, equal groups
3 Organising order of children running
4 Initial recording of time
5 Working co-operatively
6 Developing group recording methods.

Language of Math Curriculum

• Time terminology
• Length terminology and ordinal number

Literacy in Math

• Use of recording methods
• Evaluation of efficiency of recording methods
• Cardinal and ordinal numerals.

Activity 3

Short classroom activity uses a stopwatch to time how long simple actions take to complete. Main activity takes place in the outside area, preferably on the sports field. Children use a trundle wheel to measure twenty metres on the running track. Children form themselves into small groups. Each member of each group runs the marked distance and is timed by the teacher using the stopwatch.

Recording

As each child finishes they sit with their small group to make an initial record of their running times on paper. Children return to the classroom to work in their small groups. They devise recording methods that show all the times of the group members. Graphic and concrete materials are available for use. Follow-up discussion shares the recording methods of the small groups with the whole class.

MATH STRAND — NUMBER (1)

Objective: To develop math narrative 'The Take-Away Thief'

Focus: Real World → Language Math Curriculum

Activity 1

Resources
- 15–18 Cup Cakes cooked by children at a prior lesson.
- Mask and Hat for Take-Away Thief.

Activity Specific Language

Tell the children a story about the Take-Away Thief who steals cakes from the Baker's shop when no one is looking.

Set the scene for the Baker's Shop and put out the plate of cakes. Choose one child to be the Take-Away Thief. He/she creeps in and steals 2 or 3 cakes and runs off with them. The class then discuss what has happened.

Another child is selected as the Take-Away Thief and the same procedure is followed until all the cakes have disappeared.

Problem Solving Language

- How many cakes does the baker have?

  Estimate, then count to verify. (Answer 15)
- Predict: ~ How many cakes will be stolen?

  ~ Will there be more cakes or fewer cakes at the end of this game?

Language of Math Curriculum Recording

Again children should be asked to record what they have done but the recording process should not be determined.

Paul has illustrated
10 − 3 = 7
The Thief stole 3 cakes

Sample 1

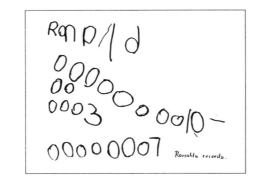

Sample 2

Matthew

Ther was a Take Away Thief
and a baker. He made Some
biscuits. Ther was ten. The take
Away thief took away five. Ther
was five more. The take away Thief
came back. He took five more. Ther
was no more.

Sample 3

MATH STRAND — NUMBER (2)

Objective: To develop a story from a set algorithm.

Focus: Literacy in Mathematics ← to the Real World.

Activity 2

Literacy in Mathematics
Set number sentence $16 - 7 = 9$.

Problem Solving Language
• Group Discussion
• What sort of story could we make up about this sum?

Real World
Sample

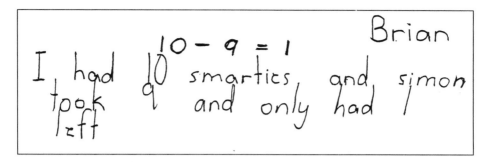

MATH STRAND — SPACE

Objective: To investigate boundaries.

Focus: Real World → Literacy of Math

Activity Specific Language
• Vocabulary associated with boundaries and pathways.
• Labels attached to road signs.
• Attributes which describe natural surroundings.
• Framing questions

Problem Solving Language:
• Estimation of time and distance.
• Predictions associated with movement along roadways, inside other boundaries and surrounding bushland.
• Decision making related to position and direction.

Language of Math Curriculum
• Terminology of position, time and length.

Literacy in Math
• Recording methods.

Activity

As part of an integrated them on 'Myself and my community', the whole group leaves school grounds via pathway. Using consensus, a decision concerning choice of pathway is made. Guesses and clarification are made about road signs, street names and house numbers. Estimation in footsteps from various points of reference are also undertaken.

Recording

1 Initial recording was oral.
2 Pictorial recordings of activity were filed.
3 Recordings using concrete play material were encouraged.
4 Further pictorial records were kept and compared to others.
5 Symbolic recordings were noted throughout the developmental process.

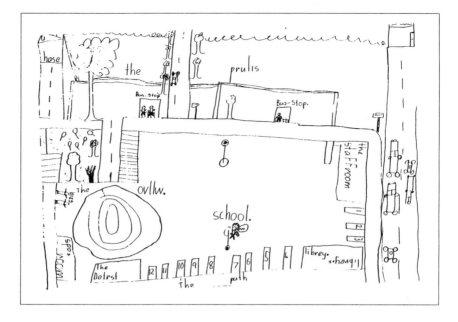

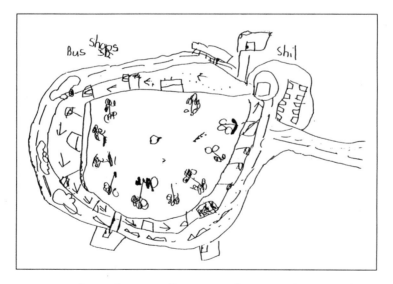

Sample recordings: Maths strand 'Space'

Conclusion

As these activities illustrate, mathematics should not be seen as computation or the need to provide the right answer. Literacy without understanding is not functional maths and the links between the two are embedded in language and concrete experience.

The mathematics curriculum should be seen as a valuable resource for desired outcomes across the grades but effective learning will depend upon how the curriculum content is interpreted, planned and applied along a logical continuum of increasing complexity.

The application of this model has provided information about our classroom practice and equally, classroom practice has helped us to explore, elaborate and refine the model to ensure that the children are able to communicate mathematically.

References

Blank, M., Rose, S., Berlin, L., (1978) *The Language of Learning*, Grune and Stratton, New York.

Gawned, S., (1989) 'The Relationship of Language Learning to Mathematics Learning', unpublished article.

Pengelly, H. (1990) Paper presented at Mt. Pleasant P.S. (WA) 1990.

Westby, C. (1985) 'Learning to Talk – Talking to Learn: Oral-Literate Language Differences' in Simon, C. (Ed.), *Communication Skills and Classroom Success*, College Hill Press.

6

Language learning and mathematics learning: a parallel approach

Mark Waters and Pam Montgomery

Waters and Montgomery show a classroom in action where children are actively processing 'real world' mathematics as they relate what they are being exposed to to their own personal experiences and backgrounds. What is interesting is that children are seen to be articulating out aloud or on paper their processing of mathematics and this overt record enables an adult to scaffold the child or the child to hear their own logic and act upon it. Waters and Montgomery also agree with Bickmore-Brand (see article this issue) that mathematics needs to have the same conditions for learning as language had for the child, and in a whole language context, not in the traditional fragmented form which is perceived as nonsense by the learners.

SUBTRACTION

Subtraction works because you rename. You rename because in subtraction, you often have a number that you can't subtract and keep the answer positive. With a number like this: **431**

                             *− **381**, you have to rename them because you can't subtract 80 from 30. So what you do is take **100** from the **400** in the hundreds column and put it with the **30** in the tens column. That makes the **30 130**. So now you can subtract **80** from **130** and keep the answer positive.*

SUBTRACTION IN GENERAL

Subtraction is the opposite to addition. You always end up with a smaller number when you subtract.

WHEN YOU USE SUBTRACTION
You use subtraction every day of your life. For instance, when you go to the supermarket and you want to get some spaghetti for tea. You have $5.00 to spend and you find some cheap spaghetti worth $3.72 and you want to find out whether you've got enough money to buy some tomato paste to put in the tomato sauce. So you subtract $3.72 from $5.00. Now you have $1.28. The tomato paste is worth $1.25. When you take them through the checkout you add $3.72 and $1.25. Then you subtract the answer from $5.00 to find out how much change you should get.

Bernadette, 12

Bernadette was a student at Strathbogie Primary school. She wrote this in mathematics time as an entry in her Mathematics Resumé. Writing this was a way of sorting what she did and didn't know about subtraction. It also became a text for informing others about subtraction.

The two of us – Mark Waters and Pam Montgomery – taught together at this school for three years. One of the major concerns at Strathbogie was to develop a quality mathematics program. To do this, research into language learning was drawn upon. The principles were then applied to the discipline of mathematics.

Pre-schoolers know lots of mathematics!

Language researchers believe that oral language learning is an exceptionally successful learning event for young children. Many researchers have analysed the environment this occurs in. They have formed theories documenting the factors contributing to this success. Can we demonstrate that an exceptional amount of mathematics learning occurs at the same time?

In the pre-school child's everyday tasks of moving, playing, feeding and dressing, much mathematical knowledge is formed. Understandings of time, length, capacity, volume, area, number and space develop. Most young children also have experience with their culture's number system and its symbolism. Consider three-year-old Sehan and his mathematical understandings emerging in a family game:

Sehan (playing 'Pick-Up-Sticks' with the family): I dot fwee.
Dad: Ye-e-ep. And I've got five.
Sehan: I want yours, Daddy.
Dad: O.K. You give me yours. (They swap sticks.)
Sehan: Daddy, I dot six.
Dad: Have you?

Sehan: Yes. (Counts the plastic sticks.) I dot one, two, fwee. I dot lots more, Daddy. (He 'fans' the sticks in one hand like playing cards and with the other hand he points to the sticks one at a time. He uses a left to right ordinal sequence.) One, two, fwee, four, six! I dot six, Daddy.
Dad: Have you?
Sehan: Yes. (He counts the sticks left to right again, fails to touch one stick mid-way but goes back and names this last in the sequence.) One, two, fwee, four, six! I dot more dan you, Daddy.

Sehan does seem to already know a lot of mathematics. He seems to know that objects can be tagged with number names, that the last number name indicates how many objects there are in the whole group, that counting is constant, that each object should be counted (thought the order of this may vary) and that some groups have more things than other groups. He has not been given formal mathematics 'lessons'. It seems reasonable to assume the same influences present in Sehan's language learning environment have made for successful mathematics learning.

What happens at school?

Ken Goodman (1986) argues that language learning in schools can either be made accessible, or interfered with, as explained in the following table:

It's easy when:	*It's hard when:*
• *It's real and natural.*	• *It's artificial.*
• *It's whole.*	• *It's broken into bits and pieces.*
• *It's sensible.*	• *It's nonsense.*
• *It's interesting.*	• *It's dull and uninteresting.*
• *It's relevant.*	• *It's irrelevant to the learner.*
• *It belongs to the learner.*	• *It belongs to someone else.*
• *It's part of a real event.*	• *It's out of context.*
• *It has a social utility.*	• *It has no social value.*
• *It has purpose for the learner.*	• *It has no discernible purpose.*
• *The learner chooses to use it.*	• *It's imposed by someone else*
• *It's accessible to the learner.*	• *It's inaccessible.*
• *The learner has the power to use it.*	• *The learner is powerless.*

We, as teachers, could see from Goodman's ideas that our mathematics program – usually worksheets and other teacher-initiated activities – was more typical of the right-hand 'It's hard when' column. We were inadvertently making mathematics learning difficult. Goodman continues to talk about (language) learning in schools:

> *With the language they've already learned, children bring to school their natural tendency to want to make sense of the world. When schools break language into bits and pieces, sense becomes nonsense, and it's always hard for kids to make sense out of nonsense. Each abstract bit and piece that is learned is soon forgotten as kids go on to further fractured fragments. In the end, they begin to think of school as a place where nothing even seems to make sense.*
>
> *That's why language learning in the real world is easy, and learning language in school should be easy but is often hard.*

We could see that mathematics learning in the real world – as in Sehan's case – was easy. Mathematics learning in our school however, was fragmented and probably nonsensical to learners. Essentially, our mathematics program lacked meaning to the learner. The challenge, as we saw it, was to maintain meaning for each child and build their mathematical knowledge from wherever it was at the time.

Meaningfulness

To meet this challenge we had to grapple with the notion of *meaningfulness*. It was obviously not possible for us to judge what aspect of mathematics was going to be immediately meaningful for each of thirty very different children.

Consider Maren, six years old, sitting at the table with her workbook and a calculator. She was punching keys industriously. Occasionally, she would write something down. She eventually approached one of the teachers:

> *Maren (flourishing the calculator): Look at this!*
> *Pam (after examining the calculator which read 2.666666): How did you get that?*
> *Maren (clears calculator and demonstrates): I went... eight... this (divide)... three... equals... two and all those sixes!*
> *Pam: If the calculator showed more numbers, those sizes would go on forever.*
> *Maren (ignoring this, clearly pursuing her own interests): I know another one. (she punches in 6 divided by 9, giving 0.666666) See?*
> *Pam: Oh, right. It's got all those sixes again.*
> *Maren: And this. (She clears the calculator and types 8, 9; then realises she has forgotten the division symbol. She clears the calculator and types 8 divided by 9 = 0.888888.) Look! It's got eights!*

Maren spent a whole week of mathematics time investigating this phenomenon. She discovered many equations which would give a recurring decimal read-out, working up from single digit numbers to two digit divisors and dividends such as 66 divided by 54 = 1.222222. She recorded every successful equation in her workbook and each day wrote, 'I used a calculator.'

Instances like this showed us that schoolchildren were capable of initiating and sustaining mathematical inquiry. More than that, Maren's mathematics had 'automatically built-in' meaningfulness. Why? We believed this was largely due to the amount of control she had over what to do and how to do it.

We began to think about allowing 'learner-control' in mathematics. Our children could competently select their own books for reading, and choose their own topics for writing. Could they also have some responsibility in planning and directing their own mathematics program? To do this, each child needed to:

• realise and articulate what they already knew of mathematics
• imagine what to find out next about mathematics.

We believed this was possible, IF the teacher supported the learner throughout these processes, and IF the environment was so saturated with the topic that the learner could easily imagine where to investigate.

Saturating the classroom with mathematics

The following are some strategies we found successful in providing this mathematics-saturated environment.

• Raise an awareness to look at your world from a mathematical perspective. What mathematical things have you done today? What mathematical potential can you see in this room? What mathematics could you learn from other people here?

• Look carefully at the range of mathematical tools around you. For instance, a ruler is an everyday measurement device. It also illustrates a base ten number line with various fractional markings.

• Regularly demonstrate your own intrigue with mathematics by pursuing an investigation which is genuinely challenging to you. For us, these were sometimes real-world necessities (filling in taxation forms, comparing superannuation scheme benefits, drawing house renovation plans) and sometimes an exploration ('I wonder how many kilometres I travel to work in a year? I wonder what Fibonacchi numbers are? I wonder how a subtraction algorithm would look if I went into negative numbers instead of renaming?').

- Allow students to bounce ideas off each other after either formal or informal sharing.
- Flood the classroom with as much quality mathematics 'literature' as possible. We made use of catalogues, bank statements, advertising brochures, maps, graphs and the like. We tried to track down books which presented mathematics as something fascinating to read about (not textbooks).
- Put curriculum documents into the learners' hands. The Victorian publications *Guidelines in Number* (Education Department, Vic., 1985) and *Mathematics Curriculum Guide Measurement* (Ministry of Education, 1981) are ideal as they are fully illustrated.
- Encourage opinionated debate about mathematics. What is mathematics? Are certain generalisations about mathematics necessarily true – do two and two always make four?
- Give open-ended challenges which focus every person in one area, but still allow for branching out.
- Talk about open and closed activities. Open activities lend themselves to more discovery.
- Show children how to write their own open-ended challenges and build up a list of 'starter' words.
- Give children summarised lists of curriculum documents, i.e. *Guidelines in Number* (Education Department, 1985) so they can nominate topics and be confronted with mathematical jargon.

Characteristics of the classroom

The following characteristics developed in the classroom. We felt they supported the main aims of (1) realising and articulating what was already known about maths and, (2) then imagining what to find out about next. They can be categorised into two distinct groups: hardcopy and activities

Hardcopy	Activity
Proposals	Sharing
Workprograms	Games
Resumés	Topics
Reports	Open and closed activities
Workbooks	

Group 1: Hardcopy

Proposals

A proposal is a way of sorting out exactly what you are going to do. We used proposals to help the learners focus their energy and plan the support and resources they might need. Proposals weren't written for everything. They were written for the longer term investigations. A lot of maths was learnt as a result of these investigations. For example, Tanya (5 years old) when trying to find out how many times she blinked in a minute, needed to: work out how to measure a minute; work out how to monitor the times she did blink; make sure that she could count as far as she needed; and find out how to record the result, which was eighteen. Her work is shown as Figure 1.

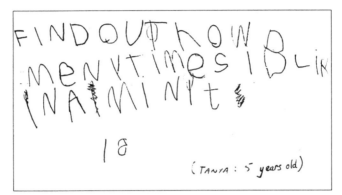

Figure 1: Tanya's proposal and answer

Workprograms

Each person, including teachers, kept a record of what they did for maths each day.

The notion of workprograms developed for a number of reasons. It was a way of keeping track of children doing lots of different things. It was also a way of legitimising lots of activity that might not have been recognised as part of maths traditionally; for example talking to your friend about constructing an investigation or browsing through maths literature to find examples of maths patterns. It was a way of encouraging accurate use of maths language. Words like algorithm, digit and vertical multiplication became commonplace. Workprograms provided another genre for the writing program. They were also used to enable children to broaden their understandings of the scope of the maths course, via periodic review. Children were encouraged to classify their maths into areas. These may have been money, addition, decimals,

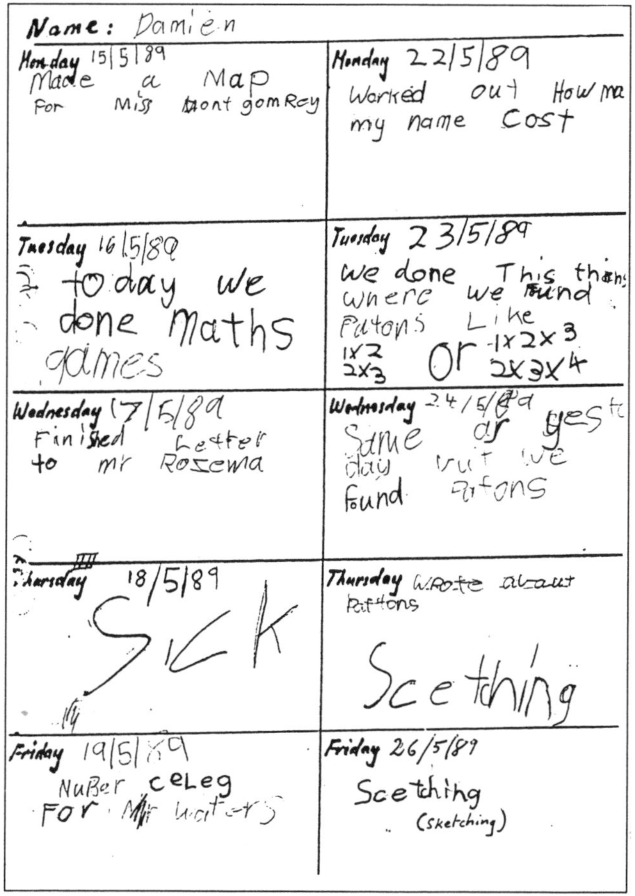

Name: Damien

Monday 15/5/89 Made a Map for Miss bont gomery	Monday 22/5/89 Worked out How me my name cost
Tuesday 16/5/89 today we done Maths games	Tuesday 23/5/89 We done This thing where we found Patons Like 1x2 2x3 3x3 Or 1x2x3 2x3x4
Wednesday 17/5/89 Finished Letter to mr Rosewa	Wednesday 24/6/89 same or yest day but we found Patons
Thursday 18/5/89 [signature] Sce tthing	Thursday wrote about Patons Sce tthing
Friday 19/5/89 Number celeg For Mr waiters	Friday 26/5/89 Sce tthing (sketching)

Fig. 2a

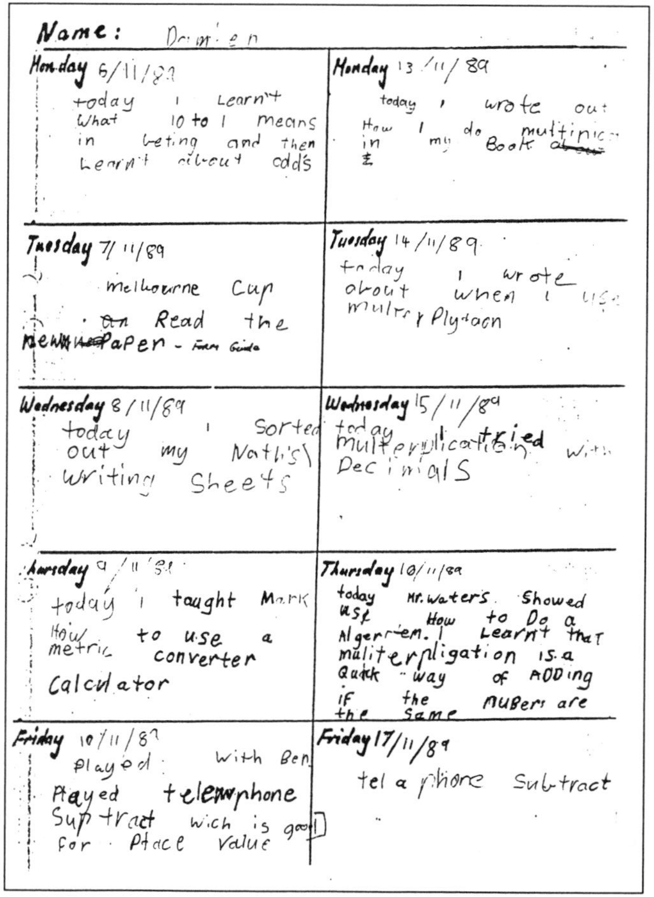

Name: Damien

Monday 6/11/89 today I Learnt What 10 to 1 means in betine and then Learnt about odds	Monday 13/11/89 today I wrote out How I do multinic in my Book
Tuesday 7/11/89 Melbourne Cup ... an Read the Newspaper - from Guido	Tuesday 14/11/89 today I wrote about when I use Multr Plytoon
Wednesday 8/11/89 today I Sorted out my Maths writing Sheets	Wednesday 15/11/89 today multiplicatiBied Decimals with
Thursday 9/11/89 today I taught Mark How to use a metric converter Calculator	Thursday 16/11/89 today Mr waters Showed me How to Do a Algerrem. I Learnt that multernligation is a quikk way of adding the nuBers are if the same
Friday 10/11/89 Played telephone with Ben Subtract for Place value	Friday 17/11/89 tel a phone subtract

Fig. 2b

Damien's workprograms six months apart

patterns, number facts, tables, etcetera. Children could then see the need to work in areas that they might not have tackled for a long time.

The developing sophistication of the workprogram was also used as evidence of growth in maths understanding. The two pages of Damien's workprogram (Figures 2a and 2b) show clear development from May through to November. He becomes far more specific in describing what he did. His facility with maths jargon is more evident. On the 16.5.89 he writes 'Today we done maths games'. On the 10.11.89 he writes 'Played with Ben. Played "Telephone Subtract" which is good for place value.' He has come to terms with writing in a small space.

In February, James' first month at school, he wrote squiggles and random mathematical symbols. When asked what they meant he told a fictional story. By October, James (now six years old) had realised that a maths workprogram should describe maths. He could describe his maths activity in recognisable maths language. He wrote the dates in recognisable numerals.

Resumés

The resumé reflects who you are as a mathematician. Like a career resumé you show your best work to date: what you would like other people to know you can do. Damien inserted his information after completing a scale drawing of the classroom (Figure 3). Lisa, seven years old, writes of her competence with multiplication. Her understandings are made evident via drawings (Figure 4): written equations, a bead frame, a hand jotting on a page, a hand grouping fingers together, a person sitting at a desk thinking.

Three areas of discussion emerged in the resumé: the method of maths, the utility of maths, and the nature of maths. In her work featured at the start of this article Bernadette clearly touches on these three areas. Firstly, she describes the algorithm she uses for subtraction. Then she touches on the mathematical nature of subtraction when she talks about subtraction being the opposite of addition. Finally, her story of the supermarket illustrates how subtraction is useful to her.

Reports

The report is for display in the room. It disseminates information between students, teachers and parents. In the giving of a report, the ideas encountered by one child were made privy to all (Figures 5 and 6). This may have entailed the reporter running everyone through an activity. With this common understanding, further discussion and exploration sometimes occurred; either individually or as a class. Some reports were three dimensional; others a combination of charts and a

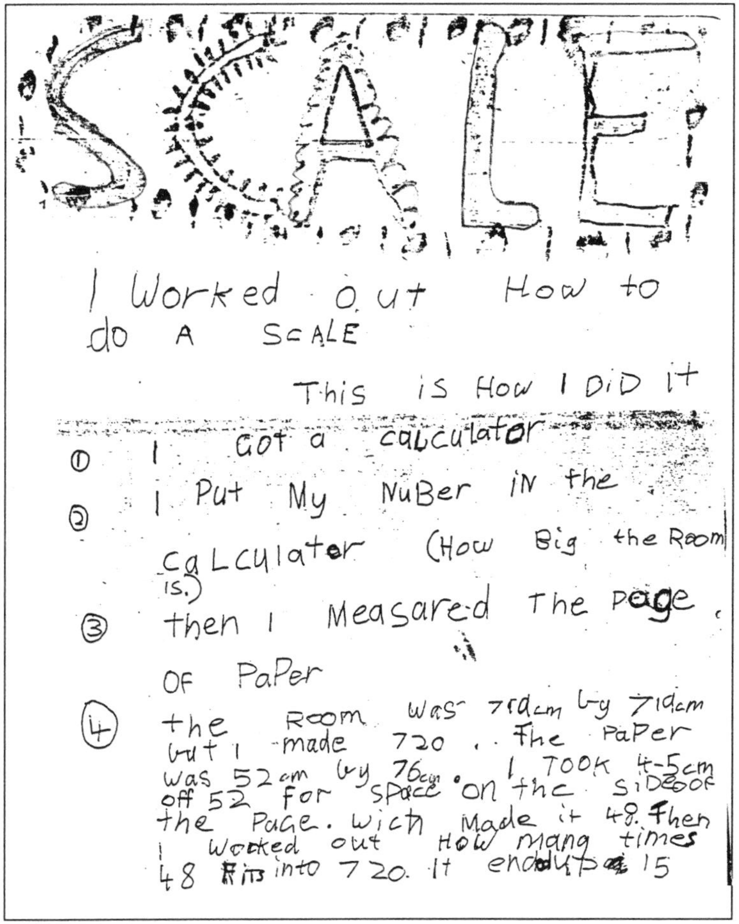

Fig. 3

I Worked Out How to do A SCALE

This is How I DID it

① I Got a calculator

② I Put My NuBer in the calculater (How Big is) the Room

③ then I Measared the page of PaPer

④ the Room was 7cm by 7cm but I made 720. The PaPer was 52cm by 76cm I Took off 5cm off 52 for space on the side of the Page. Wich made it 48 then I worked out How many times 48 fits into 720. It ended up as 15

Fig. 3

Fig. 4

I Do Like how to KNow MULTiPLion this

Example
$4 \times 5 = 20$
$1 \times 5 = 2$

$\begin{array}{r} 5 \\ \times\, 2 \\ \hline 10 \end{array}$

Fig. 4

Resumés

RESULTS

I burnt two matches and got two different times. The first time took 31 seconds to burn and the second one took 33 second. I multiplied them both by 50 because there is approximately 50 matches in a box. the first one equalled 1650 (27 min. 30 sec). The second one equalled 1650 (25 min 30 sec).

What I planned to do

1) Get -a stop watch
       -a pair of tweezers
       -a cup of water
       -a box of matches

2) Light one match. Hold it up straight and wait until it burns to the bottom. Then drop it in the water.

How I Did it.

1) I got a pair of tweezers.
       a cup of water
       a stop watch
       a box of matches

2) I asked Roslyn to time me. I lit the match and turned it upside down for a second to catch alight. When it got to the middle. I turned it upside down to keep it going. I turned it on its side for three seconds. Then I turned it upside down again to finish it.

Fig. 5: Bernadette's report

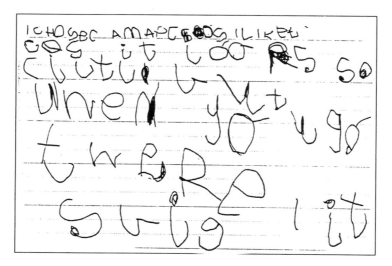

Fig 6: James' report

talk. The examples from Bernadette and James were chosen because of size and ease of duplication.

Workbooks

The workbook is where all the jottings, small calculations, and drafts go. This was viewed a little like a writers' journal. It was a clipboard for experimenting. It was non-judged/risk free. Loretta's workbook showed a non-intelligible conglomerate that meant little to anyone but Loretta. Eventually it developed into an entry for her Resumé.

Group 2: Activities

Sharing

Sharing is a mentality. Initially a very formal session was timetabled, during which a lot of attitudes were modelled by the teachers – attitudes like finding an interest in what another person was doing, and striving to understand that person's intentions rather than assuming what you thought they meant and imposing your own ideas. Body language when listening was also spoken about. Everyone was encouraged to question any statement that they didn't understand.

Eventually there were more spontaneous sharing times. The small conquests were celebrated between children and teachers without waiting for a sharing time. The timetabled sharing sessions became more of a group stocktake.

Games

We had a timetabled session where all people were involved in selecting and playing a variety of games which had mathematical content. This was a time to highlight the social and aesthetic profiles of mathematics. The children were encouraged to reflect on the mathematical content in whatever game they elected.

Topics

At times, a broad topic was given for all to study. This gave a common group direction for discussion – a little like discussing a novel read by all in literature. Within the topic, children covered the ground that was necessary for them to further their own understanding. There was an implicit understanding that all people would move into areas of the topic they were unsure of. For instance, whilst working on the topic 'Addition', Shannon, aged seven, grappled with vertical addition. He had seen older children using this. Meanwhile Damien, aged ten, was learning to add numbers with decimals. Mark, also ten, was learning to add fractions with different denominators.

Open and closed activities

Children were involved in discussions concerning how open or closed various mathematics investigations were. Although we sometimes used open-ended challenges, there was still credence given to closed investigations, i.e. seeing how much a litre of water weighs. The answer is reasonably closed, the way of finding out is quite open. We spent time showing how an activity which looked closed could be 'opened up' to become more exploratory.

Writing

It is obvious that writing was a pervasive element within the mathematics program. Writing was used as a major strategy for helping learners know more of what they already know and what they might find out about next. The generative nature of writing is also recognised: that is, during the writing act new thought will be created. We drew strongly on the work of Frank Smith and his beliefs about the power of writing (Smith, 1982).

Demonstrations

Child to child

We were aware each child's involvement in their mathematics task was potentially a demonstration for all other children. This was particularly critical for younger children sitting alongside older children and watching them at work.

Teacher to child

Just as whole language classrooms see teachers demonstrating real reading and writing, we felt our mathematics classroom should see teachers demonstrating their learning of and involvement in mathematics. Sometimes our demonstrations were exploratory, sometimes they were expository, such as, 'This is how I tackle a vertical addition algorithm'.

Whatever the type, we believe these agenda came through:

1. Your belief about the nature of mathematics drives any demonstration. For instance, if you believe in the objective reality of mathematics, then your demonstration of an algorithm will probably endorse its immutability. If you believe that mathematics is socially constructed, then your demonstration will probably use an investigative approach; eventually settling on the most efficient way for you.

2. Your attitude to both mathematics and learning is critical. If demonstrations carry positive messages such as, 'Isn't this idea intriguing?' I don't know much about this. I think I'll find out.' 'I think I've nearly got the hang of this!' then learners begin to reflect these values. Mathematics can be seen as a fascinating, luring pursuit. Learning mathematics can be exciting and intrinsically rewarding. Like lots of other learning, this can require hard work, but hard work needn't be automatically equated with negative ideas such as tedium. On the subject of hard work, we often referred to an attitude of 'having commitment to the task', which had a more positive connotation.

3. The content of your demonstrations can affect the content the children choose to investigate. At one stage, children were becoming so involved in number and measurement work that the mathematics of shape was being neglected. Our next few demonstration sessions used shape as the content to renew interest in this area.

We were involved in all hardcopy characteristics of the classroom. Figures 7a and 7b show two examples – a teacher's maths workprogram and a teacher's proposal.

Teacher to teacher

The points stressed above regarding the agenda of a demonstration seem to carry extra weight when they occur in a teacher to teacher demonstration. It was one thing to discuss the nature of multiplication with a group of children, but when this became a debate between teachers in front of the class, its credibility was absolute.

As a school program

It was not an easy task to synthesise all these ideas into a short statement which would act as a school-based document. Eventually we arrived at this.

1 Daily immersion in maths, via:
- real world applications • investigations
- maths reading • maths writing
- games • open-ended challenges
- being exposed to the scope of mathematics
- drawing attention to the mathematical nature of our world.

2 Opportunities to hear about quality maths activity from:
- peers • professionals

Fig. 7b: A teacher's proposal

MATHS INVESTIGATION

I will cost out this year's school camp to Chiltern. I need to consider the following monetary aspects of the trip.

TRAVEL Need to find distances from strathbogie to chiltern and then to places we intend visiting.

FOOD Need to plan the menu for three days.

ENTRANCE FEES Need to plan and book the venues and activities.

ACCOMMODATION Find out whether chiltern P.S. expect any remuneration for using their facilities.

Fig. 7a: A teacher's workprogram

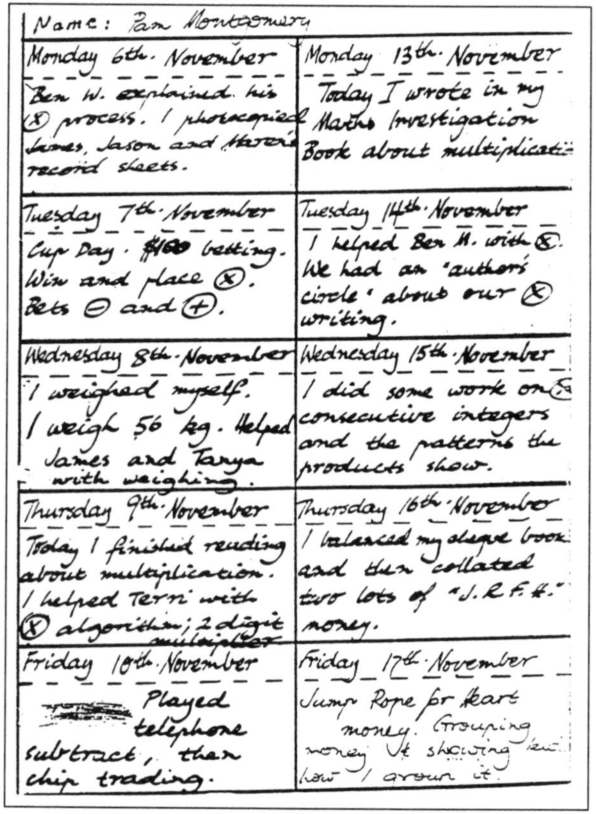

3 Opportunities to see peers, adults and teachers in the process of engaging in maths investigations.

4 Encouragement of community caring:
   - celebrating success   • giving help when needed
   - recognition of, and support through, frustrations.

5 Encouragement of risk taking.

6 Children being expected to take ownership over their learning.

7 Interaction with peers and others to give and receive honest help.

8 Highlighting of strategies that help children gain control of mathematics.

9 Engagement in relevant, meaningful tasks (mainly through child choice).

10 Time to pursue what is important – time to finish investigations which may take days or weeks.

Lastly

Why did this classroom work? We tried to isolate the one most powerful element to answer this. We couldn't! Instead we settled on two closely connected ideas.

Firstly, each child is respected for the world they're creating at that moment in time. We approach the children to teach us what they're learn–ing, not to test what they known. The norm is: each child works on the brink of their own understanding. Obviously there is intrigue and delight with what they discover or create.

Secondly, each teacher is working on the brink of their own understanding and each takes delight in their own breakthroughs.

References

Education Department, (1985) *Guidelines in Number* Government Printer, Melbourne.

Goodman, K. (1986) *What's Whole in Whole Language?* Portsmouth, NH: Heinemann.

Ministry of Education, (1981) *Mathematics Curriculum Guide Measurement* Government Printer, Melbourne.

Smith, Frank (1986) *Writing and the Writer* Hillsdale, NJ: L. Erlbaum.

7

The mathematics-language connection

Noelene Reeves

Reeves confronts the issue that mathematics is rarely integrated into language programs. Research supports that language is essential for teaching and learning - in generating, comprehending and expressing mathematical ideas and mathematical knowledge. Reeves recognises the need for classroom talk to not only be with rather than at or to children, but to manipulate concrete situations. This will provide the context from which the language was derived. With this comes the need for teachers to be aware of the purpose behind doing mathematics. Teachers need to be overt about the language of problem-solving and the associated linguistic features of the register so that it can connect with the child's own schema and developing understandings.

In this essay, I aim to show why language is the essential vehicle for transmitting and understanding mathematics in school, for turning experience into thinking and learning. More importantly, I aim to explore specific language acquisition and development without which the formal aspects of mathematics cannot be appreciated.

Introduction

I once attended a session at a reading conference given cooperatively by a university lecturer in language and language acquisition and a classroom teacher about a new and exciting 'total language programme' in a K–1 classroom. It *was* exciting; oral language, reading and writing development were carefully planned and integrated with social and physical sciences, literature, art and craft and so on in a very satisfying way. The ideas and experiences were interrelated with the ways of expressing and recording them. There were many examples of the

children's work and there was a video of the children being inter-
viewed which showed their greater awareness of language. They were
extremely articulate and confident. What they thought about reading
and writing showed a developing clarity of purpose and understanding
of process.

'And where is the maths?' I asked. 'How do you develop the mathematics component into your total language programme?'

The lecturer stared at me for a moment and looked a little nonplused.
'We haven't included maths,' he said. 'You can't, can you?'

'Why not?'

'Well, mathematics is mathematics and language is language.'

'What happens in maths, then?'

'The Principal comes in to do the maths whilst the teacher goes to
another class for language activities.'

I was no longer so impressed with the 'total' language programme
and very disappointed that the mathematics/language connection had
not been made by obviously gifted teachers.

It seems that mathematics is so often put along-side language in a
separate box or put in the 'too hard' basket by many teachers who fail
to see the significance of a language focus for the learning and teaching
of mathematics, other than perhaps the importance of understanding
terminology. This essay will advocate that mathematics education in
schools is fundamentally a language activity. It is through language
and not activities or materials that mathematics is learned. This propo-
sition, however, needs some explanation and justification before ex-
amination.

Learning: the essential context

The previous statement may appear to contradict mathematics educators of the past ten years or so, who have rightly pointed out that
mathematics is NOT talk and chalk, but a material-based, investigatory
activity. It may appear to be suggesting that activity-based mathematics and problem-solving approaches or hands-on type situations are in
question so let me hasten to add that it does not, nor should it. The
advocates of such an approach have never assumed that mathematics
is learned in silence. Indeed, 'discussion' is part of the approach.

The role of language in the growth and understanding of mathematical ideas has long been recognised. The use of oral language as an
essential component of any mathematics education has been advo-
cated by mathematics educators everywhere, emphasised by professional committees of enquiry, (such as the Cockroft Committee in the

UK) and, of course, included in Australian mathematics syllabuses by local education department officers involved with curriculum development.

What is needed now is to focus on what is being said (and written) and by whom and why. It is easy to say that language is important. It is more difficult to make explicit at the classroom level just what language is essential for teaching and learning, and what part language plays in generating, comprehending and expressing mathematical ideas and mathematical knowledge. It is always assumed that teachers and students will talk about mathematics but just what is being said and for what purpose is rarely discussed. The issue needs to be teased out a great deal further to understand the role of language that turns planned experience into mathematical competency.

The role of experience

The experience to be talked about is equally significant. In 1986, ARA took as the theme for its national conference *Text and Context* in recognition that language usage is always contextual, relying on content, purpose and audience. Young children's mathematical thinking is also contextual. The work of researchers such as Piaget, and more recently, Hughes, Gelman or Van Den Brink, has confirmed again and again that young children can only think about and comprehend mathematics as it relates to specific contexts. Abstraction and abstract reasoning develop with time, constructed from experience. The creation of contexts to provide quality experience is what multi-sensory mathematics education has been advocating for several years, setting up experiences that are relevant and appropriate to young children whence mathematical information can be gleaned. That is why materials, activity and investigations are so important. The child has to have experienced something potentially mathematical to recall, visualise and talk about. The content has to be real to the child. Put differently, it is not possible to talk mathematics if the child cannot manipulate or imagine a concrete situation that reflects the processes and products of mathematics.

The desire to communicate

Language stems from the desire to communicate and its development depends on someone wanting to listen and respond. So it follows that mathematical language also stems from a real desire children have to want to talk to an appreciative audience, and its development on wanting to listen to a competent user. Unless a classroom climate enables talk to be *with*, rather than *at* or *to* children, language development, including mathematical language, will not flourish. It is not possible to talk mathematics unless there is a genuine desire to communicate and this cannot happen in a vacuum.

It is TEACHER TALK + CHILD TALK = MATHEMATICS.

School, language development and mathematical thought

It needs to be further emphasised just how fundamental context is to text and language development before exploring the idea that it is the language that accompanies the experience that determines mathematical learning, not necessarily the materials or the situation.

Young children's learning before school is overwhelmingly contextual, making sense of what their five senses tell them and also what is happening to them. Their language learning is an interrelated accompaniment to their physical experiences, and its development is socially determined. Children are fast, active learners in their natural learning style – they have to be! When children enter formal education they are still very much reliant on sensory information to supplement their growing, but still comparatively limited, language skills.

Mathematics is not a physical experience but a creation of the human mind, a mental processing and reviewing of reality as it relates to space, time and quantity, indeed, high level thinking. It is abstract, not context bound. But, because of immaturity and lack of experience, the only way a young child can understand and appreciate mathematical information is to have it presented in contextual form appropriate to their level of experience. Presented abstractly, it will be learnt by rote, repeated but not necessarily understood and certainly not transferred or applied to new situations. Hence, our primary concern as teachers of mathematics is to make sure that children experience situations where ideas and relationships about space, time and quantity can be physically manipulated, imagined and talked about. Indeed, children have to DO mathematics before they can THINK mathematics.

Experienced teachers can recall situations in the 'old days' when mathematical ideas were being discussed in the abstract for the benefit of the few whilst the majority of students stared at the symbols and listened to the words without comprehending in the least what, for example, a percentage was, or why you divided by a fraction by turning it upside down and multiplying, or why, when multiplying by fractions, the answer was less than the number you started with! It is now accepted that talk alone is not the way to teach and learn.

The role of language in learning mathematics

Now it is time, therefore, to make the opposite assumption about any mathematics classroom. The fundamental component that has to be taken for granted is that talk will only be going on in the context of the appropriate activity, that the children are DOING for themselves and that the activity needs the child talk and the teacher talk to turn the doing into thinking mathematics. Then talk plays two vital roles:

1. The first is to link children's experience to socially accepted ideas which learners have to discover anew for themselves so that the ideas become personal knowledge. Call it 'social transmission' perhaps. It includes counting and number, measurement and money, the numeration system... the content of a mathematics syllabus. It is a 'sharing' of information available to all members of a society as a basis for social interaction. It is what makes this society a 'numerate' society.

Children depend on a knowledgeable 'other' to provide this view of the world. It is cultural as well as social and is learnt through language and feedback. A child depends on the language of self and others for the social construction of mathematical ideas. No matter what situations children experience, they are told how to view them mathematically by someone who already knows – parents or teachers – and are thus, to varying degrees, inducted into the social experience.

2. The second is to generate creative thinking in individuals, to encourage different ideas and problem-solving skills for intellectual development and personal satisfaction. It is this aspect that prepares children for the abstract nature of the discipline. It is this aspect that makes the study of mathematics an ongoing, dynamic field of endeavour still to benefit society in ways not yet thought about.

The personal, individual resources that a child has to draw on depend on the range of experience, opportunities for challenge and the value attached to the endeavour. There is growing evidence that teacher talk plays a determinant role in how children will think; that a teacher's own mathematical understanding, the language a teacher uses and the nature of the discourse can enlarge or restrict a child's view, can blinker or expand a child's thinking.

The quality of the talk will determine the quality of the learning and the degree of success and satisfaction experienced by the learners. This is to take up the theme of another ARA national conference on *Language and Learning*. Children learn mathematics when the subject is the topic of conversation, and children learn the language of and for mathematics in just the same way. Mathematics language development is no different from any other language learning process: it just happens to be about particular ideas and processes. It needs the same conditions for learning as those described by Cambourne or Montessori; there has to be a purpose, a model, encouragement, respect, feedback, and time to perfect.

There is, therefore, both a social and individual language resource required for mathematics learning and teaching. The challenge for educators is to understand its composition and to develop ways of developing a rich resource.

The mathematics register

Is there anything special about the language of the mathematics classroom? The answer is decidedly YES. It has to be both product and process oriented with precision.

When I first started thinking about a project called 'Mathematics in the Early Years', several years ago, I talked with many teachers about the way they taught mathematics and about their successes, but also a great deal about their fears and feelings of inadequacy in dealing with the subject. They were very frank and honest, admitting that thinking of things to do with the children was no real problem – there were numerous excellent resources available to assist them – but thinking about what to say and feeling confident that what they were saying was really bringing out the purpose of the activity WAS a problem. They asked many questions to which I had no really satisfying answers. Why, for example, is sorting and classifying so fundamental? Why make patterns with materials? Why let children invent their own problem-solving strategies? Where were the links to 'real' mathematics they were supposed to be forging?

I took myself back on a voyage of rediscovery of fundamentals and decided that, stripped of all detail, mathematics was very simple. It amounted to the mind dealing with information about space, time and quantity in three ways: grouping, ordering and changing. This processed information is then used for solving problems.

I also decided that we had developed an English language register to communicate all of this. Some of the words were kept solely for mathematics, some we used every day in alternative situations. The words used only in mathematics, or reserved for special mathematical meanings, we think of as mathematical terms, or formal language. The rest we might refer to as natural language. The register is made up of both with the terminology used in meaning-making discourse.

Grouping talk

Sometimes we focus on making and labelling groups and sub-groups. This is where the sorting and classifying comes in but so too does allocation and unitising. We give language labels to properties of objects and sets of objects. As the groups and attributes become more complex and precise, so the labels become more formal and less open to choice.

box, ball cube…
sharp, straight, round…
long, short, heavy…
centimetre, gram…
lot, many, piece, three, mob, a hundred…

One of these labels is number, the cardinal aspect.

perimeter, circle, polygon…
curve, arc, rightangle, plane, solid, invariant, dimension…
area, mass, volume, capacity…
minutes, degrees, litres…
primes, multiples, triangular number, integers, googol, fraction, place-value…

Ordering talk

Sometimes we are more interested in the relationships between the groups and describe the many, many links that can be made. Comparing and ordering, seriating according to an attribute, setting out in a regular fashion, making patterns and tables all rely on creating or noticing relationships between objects (including self) and sets of objects. The language is there to describe the various degrees of relationships, some precise, others a bit woolly. The ordinal aspect of number is an element of the language of precision.

in, on, under, between, next…
smoother, fits, matches…
longer, heavier, longest…
more, most, first, last…
equal to, more than, difference between, the same…
the same size, the same amount…

The fascinating part comes when relationships are established between relationships, and the mind plays with relationships between ideas. There is language for that as well, sophisticated and demanding.

Changing talk

But change seems to interest us most and we like to know what is going to happen if we alter the groupings or the relationships and whether we can change them back or not. Describing change and predicting outcomes with certainty is where the basic number facts fit in. The mathematical operations of addition, subtraction, multiplication and division are certainly transformations but they do not always refer to number.

> *put in, go past, get between, go next…*
> *roll, stack, pat, squeeze, slide, turn, turn over…*
> *add, put together, collect, gather…*
> *take, cut off, break, take away…*
> *repeat, another two, pairs, lots of…*
> *share, divide, spread, regroup…*

We can talk about all of these physical and mental processes in English and in other languages as well. Even more amazingly, we can depict them pictorially or write about them in signs and symbols and so can others who are non-English speaking. There is mutual comprehension through the representations even though speaking another tongue. Formal mathematics becomes a language in its own right.

So this is what is so special about the role of language in the mathematics classroom. Teachers have to know and model the register, embed the formal aspect in natural discourse, immerse children in meaning-making talk, encourage them to initiate and respond. It is from the teacher's language that children will appreciate ideas and develop skills. As they learn to talk about ideas in relation to experience, they learn the language of mathematics.

Mathematical discourse and metacognition

A parallel responsibility in the teaching and learning of mathematics is for children to learn to think, to think logically and to solve problems. Engaging a child's mind is easier said than done, but there are at least two ways I know of that work: using a child's curiosity and using a child's desire to communicate.

Finding out and telling what you did, know, thought, saw… requires the child to think. Framing the task, asking questions, raising possibilities, showing genuine interest in the problem and the solution, asking to be informed, listening in order to take the child that little bit further in the thinking process, are the skills of mathematics teaching primarily dependent on classroom discourse.

The discourse must be meta-cognitive, to create the awareness of thought: to encourage predictions, hypothesizing, if/then situations; what if, why, what would happen, what did happen, how did you know, how did you find out, what do you think, what do you recall, what could happen, how many ways, what other ways... The possibilities are endless but the important point is that the discourse is a conversation, not a quiz or a test. It can be done with groups and classes as well as individual children. This kind of discourse stimulates curiosity about the task and promotes reasoning even if the reasoning is not always obvious to the participating adult. It seems to me that this is what is meant by 'discussion'.

But meaning-making of discourse between a 'novice' and an 'expert', to use Cambourne's terms, does more than this. It is not just an interesting conversation to start or finish off an activity. It has to play a central role in intellectual development.

Using discussion purposefully, a teacher will aim to clarify meaning. What exactly does 'divide' mean. Discourse can clarify mathematical meanings of words with other connotations: table, face, relations... These words used in context allow the child to absorb terminology, to make meaning, to comprehend.

Talk enlarges the register. Given language and information in the context of interest and/or curiosity may give children something new to think about even though not fully understood. How else do children meet new language or new ideas and realise that there could be other possibilities, that there is more to learn? A mathematics teacher is also a story teller, an opener of windows, a provider of new ideas.

- Talk refines meaning. How big is 'big'?
- Talk gives precision to known terms. What exactly is 'half' or how long is a 'minute'?
- Talk gives pictures for the mind, for comprehension or for problem solving. It is possible to use fiction as well as fact to illustrate or stimulate a mathematical understanding.

By making mathematics a part of a total language programme that focusses on developing thinking skills and metacognition in addition to vocabulary, children will be given the language FOR mathematics that will take them beyond the functional to the creative satisfactions of the discipline. It also gives the subject a 'knowledge-worth', of intrinsic social importance that becomes a pleasure to learn rather than a punishment.

Conclusion

There is still a great deal more to be found out about the relationship between language and mathematics learning, the importance of individual language resources and the impact of classroom discourse on concept development. But at this point in time there is no doubt that there is a fundamental connection. Language is central to the psychology and sociology of mathematics education.

Activities and materials make mathematics for the eyes and the hands, but

TEACHER TALK AND CHILD TALK MAKES MATHEMATICS

in the minds of the learners.

Children's mathematical development is a task for minds, dependent on listening to the language models provided in the context of mathematical experience and having the opportunity to talk and experiment with language themselves.

In the home and then in the pre-school, oral language is the focus, but it has been my experience to note that when the reading/writing mode is introduced there is a sharp reduction in the emphasis given to oral language development. The oral mode should never be supplanted by the additional mode, only complemented; and, given encouragement, children will relate in words and writing, rather than symbols, their observations and understandings. To me, this is an essential link between experience, talk and formal representation. Without a firm foundation of the language OF mathematics and language FOR mathematics, the symbols can confuse and inhibit mathematical development.

In this essay I have argued that mathematical comprehension and skill development stems from a language/experience base. We have to consciously make sure children are given that essential platform for mathematics. In my view, the only way to ensure the quality of mathematics education children deserve is to keep talking with children from a sound mathematical knowledge base and be patient, for ideas take time to formulate and language takes time to control. Mathematics education is a classroom-based language experience and teachers are children's life-line to the language-mathematics connection.

8

Reading and writing in mathematics

Mollie MacGregor

MacGregor investigates the reading demands when grappling with the mathematical register. She highlights the difficulties students have when processing mathematical language. MacGregor used student examples from non-English speaking backgrounds. These students have difficulty both talking and writing about their mathematical concepts or processing. MacGregor acknowledges the handicap that exists for speakers of non-standard English, regardless of their race, and that it is teachers' responsibility to assist pupils to become literate in the mathematics register.

Constructing meaning from mathematical texts

In old books of puzzles and riddles you will find the following:

Brothers and sisters have I none.
This man's father is my father's son.

To work out the relationship between the 'I' and 'this man' of the riddle requires more effort than reading usually involves. Why should this be so? There are no technical terms or difficult words in the riddle. Everybody knows what brothers, sisters, sons and fathers are. The statements are short. There are no embedded clauses, logical connectives, negatives or passive constructions, all of which can make ordinary language difficult to read. The problem refers to human beings (*somebody's father, my father* and *somebody's son*), and not to any of the abstract entities of mathematics. It should be easy to imagine the people referred to and sort out who they are. However anyone tackling this riddle for the first time finds that it takes organised thinking (and perhaps pencil-and-paper as well) to work out who 'this man' is. It appears that the strategies normally used for reading and constructing meaning are insufficient.

In most everyday reading, we don't need to be aware of each word or of its position on the page relative to others. The construction of meaning is strongly guided by our knowledge of the particular context and our general knowledge of how the world works. Theories of human language processing (see, for example, Bever, 1970; Forster, 1979; Wanner & Maratsos, 1978) propose that very little analysis of grammatical relationships and word order is carried out in ordinary circumstances. For example, the collection of words *tram conductors, union officials, meeting, midday, deadlocked,* and *continue,* presented in any order, tells newspaper readers that, as they had anticipated, a dispute involving tram conductors is unresolved. There is only one likely way that tram conductors, a meeting, and midday are related, so there is no need for the reader to attend to the order in which they are mentioned or to the prepositions *in* and *at* linking them in the text. Since there are no alternative meanings that would make sense in the context, it is not necessary to pay attention to grammatical structure.

In the *this man's father* riddle, the key elements are: brother, sister, myself, this man, father, son. There are many possible ways that these elements could be related (*this man's brother, my son, my father's father,* and many more) and they would all make equally good sense. To solve the riddle, the reader has to choose one of the key elements and use it as a reference point for the others. The functional relations between words in the sentence, and the order of words, are crucial to meaning. Careful attention has to be given to the direction of one-way relations such as *father of.* The word *is* indicates that the reader should look for equivalent names, and perhaps substitute one for the other. We will see that the analytic reading strategies required to make sense of the riddle are the same as the strategies required for reading in mathematics.

If we look at a typical statement of mathematics text, for example:

> *The volume (V) cubic centimetres of a spherical cap of height (h) centimetres cut off from a sphere of radius r centimetres by a plane distant (5 − h) centimetres from the centre is the sum of two terms...*

we see that it has the structural characteristics of the riddle. As in the riddle, all elements in the statement refer to each other. The reader has to find the fundamental reference, *sphere,* and work out how the other elements relate to it. The information has to be broken down into a set of simple propositions, in an appropriate order, such as: *There is a sphere. The radius of the sphere is r cm. A plane cuts the sphere. The distance from the centre of the sphere to this plane is (r − h) centimetres.* As in the riddle, the direction of one-way relations is important; *(r − h)* is not the same as

$(h - r)$, for example. The word *is* indicates an equivalence of two expressions. Notice that the reader needs special knowledge of the functions of prepositions and the ways they are used in technical text. For example, the phrase *sphere of radius r* has to be interpreted as giving information about *the radius of* a sphere; the preposition *of* has been used in an unusual way. The reader also needs familiarity with the compressed language register of the mathematician. For example, the phrase *a plane distant (r − h) centimetres* tells the reader that there is a plane to be considered, and gives information about the distance of this plane from a particular point and the measure of the distance in centimetres.

What causes problems when students read mathematical texts?

Like the riddle, mathematical statements need to be analysed into their structural components and these components then need to be related to each other. Major stumbling blocks for students trying to read mathematical and other technical text are:
• not being aware that analytic reading is necessary;
• lacking experience and skill in analytic reading;
• unfamiliarity with the standard uses of prepositions.

As Clements (1984) has pointed out, children are likely to have more language-related difficulties in the mathematics classroom than they experience anywhere else. Teachers may not have thought about the level of reading skills necessary for comprehending technical text. Traditional school mathematics was designed for children who were learning English and Latin grammar, and who were proficient in English as their mother-tongue. In Australian schools today there are large numbers of children who are learning English as a second language and many Australian-born children from non English-speaking backgrounds who may not be familiar with formal standard English. It can no longer be assumed by mathematics teachers that their pupils have acquired sufficient syntactic awareness and analytic reading skills in English to cope with the register of mathematical text. **Learning how to read mathematical text needs to be part of the mathematics curriculum.**

For many students in school, learning mathematics consists of finding out 'what you are supposed to do' in particular contexts, and 'writing the answer'. They are rarely asked to explain why they have chosen a particular procedure, why it makes sense, or what information is provided by their answers. If asked to write an explanation, many students don't know what to write. They see no purpose in writing, since they have not had the experience of using words and mathematical notation as a tool for mathematical thinking. They believe that clever people do maths in their heads, or occasionally on the back of an envelope where they scribble down a few numbers that need to be remembered. They have not discovered that *we find out what we think when we write, and in the process we put thinking to work* (Smith, 1986, p. 35).

Expressing mathematical ideas on paper

Writing about mathematical ideas is even harder than reading about them. To talk or write about abstract concepts and relationships, and perhaps also to fully understand them, depends on using carefully structured language. Many students do not have the linguistic skills necessary for clarifying and expressing mathematical ideas. For example, a group of primary teacher trainees had considerable difficulty trying to explain the associative property of addition. Here are some of their attempts:

> *If there is group of number is does not matter with (sic) order they are the anser (sic) is the same (sic)*
>
> *No matter how the equation is done it will always answer.*
>
> *It can be broken down to equal the same as both equations.*
>
> *The associative property of addition is the addition method which breaks up whole numbers in order to make addition simple.*
>
> *Doesn't matter which way you grap (sic) them will still be the same amant (sic).*

It is clear that these students do not have the necessary language competence for writing about logical relationships. They may be able to make use of the associative property in particular instances of simple computation, without knowing exactly what it is. They are unable to use language to explore partly-formed understanding and refine ideas. Their gaps in linguistic knowledge may impose limits on their conceptual knowledge and inhibit the processes of deductive reasoning. They need experience in using language in order to realise their potential as learners and, later, as teachers.

The value of writing in mathematics classes

Writing tasks in mathematics are valuable for both teacher and learner. Misconceptions and gaps in understanding are exposed when the learner tries to write a definition or an explanation. Non-standard grammatical forms and limited language skills, which may pass unnoticed in speech, become immediately apparent. Concepts that were previously partly formed at a non-verbal level can be explored, extended, classified, communicated and verified. The learner is engaged in high-level thinking and the active construction of meaning. **The value of writing in mathematics classes as a learning technique deserves attention from practising teachers and researchers.**

The use of non-standard English and its penalties

In the *National Policy on Languages* (1987), Joseph Lo Bianco stated that

> *...technologically-based developments will continue to change society and... language will assume even greater importance. In a society becoming rapidly more complex, skilled use of language will increasingly become an instrument of empowerment and social participation* (p. 79).

He pointed out that there are *'severe social and economic penalties'* (p. 81) for students who fail to learn the academic and formal registers of English.

The use of non-standard English, by teachers and by students, is likely to be a severe handicap to learning in mathematics and science. There are large numbers of young Australians who are growing up with non-standard varieties of English. In any multicultural society, it is inevitable that grammatical forms of the common language become simplified in informal, unwritten discourse. In Australian vernacular at the present time, for example, prepositions are often omitted entirely in simple statements about objects and events. For example in 'Railway Dialect', a train *'departs platform 8'* and *'stops all stations'*; in 'TV Dialect', a programme *'premieres Tuesday 7 pm'*; in 'Supermarket Dialect', a store manager says *'thank you for shopping Coles'*. The words *from, at,* and *on* are omitted without any perceived loss of communication. The context makes meanings obvious. In mathematics, however, each preposition has its particular function and must not be ignored.

The place of vernacular English

The suggestion that non-standard languages, such as localised vernaculars or dialects, may interfere with learning is sometimes taken to imply that one form of language is inferior to another. Consequently, according to Orr (1987), investigations into the interaction between students' non-standard language use and learning are generally avoided, since they might be seen as an investigation of deficiencies rather than differences. It has been suggested (Trudgill, 1975) that teachers can show that they respect a student's non-standard vernacular while still teaching the standard form of the language as an alternative form to be used for particular purposes. Access to the standard form of a language is the right of every student. Corson (1989), in an article on language policies for schools, pointed out that schools must work towards widening children's mastery over language in all its forms and functions. An effective way for students to gain competence in language usage is by writing.

ESL and the vocabulary demands of the mathematical register

For students who are learning English as a second language, the most difficult words to deal with are the words that designate specific relationships between parts of sentences. Even when necessary vocabulary and word-order have been mastered, the use of auxiliary words is hard to learn. The following example showing misuse of *from* and *on* comes from a short essay written by a 15-year-old Yugoslav girl, who learned English at an intensive language centre in Melbourne. She is describing her first days in high school.

> *I did my maths very well, maybe better from (sic) most of the girls in the class… It was a new feeling when I though[t] on a second language.*

Misuse of the words *from* and *on* does not cause the reader to misinterpret the message, since we know what she means. In mathematics, however, the wrong preposition can make meanings obscure or change them completely. A student teacher of non English-speaking background (NESB) in a Dip.Ed. essay wrote:

> *…finding common factors from two numbers e.g. the factors of 7 and 12 are 3 and 4.*

This student's use of the word *from* in the context is non-standard, and it is clear that the concept of *common factors* is not understood. Another NESB student in the class, also writing about common factors, used the preposition *between*. She wrote:

> *…the common factor between 3, 9, 12*

instead of the conventional *common factor of 3, 9, and 12*. She may know what a common factor is, but is likely to have trouble in talking about it with pupils.

The word *between* was misused by some students in referring to ratios. For example, a student wrote *the ratio between objects*. His use of the word *between* suggests that he may be unsure whether ratio is a multiplicative relation or one that describes a difference between quantities. His use of the word *objects* suggests that he may not clearly distinguish an object from its attributes and from measures of these attributes. The misconception of ratio as a difference may also be seen in the following sentences:

> *There are five more of the amount of dogs than cats.*
>
> *The number of dogs are of a greater margin than the number of cats.*
>
> *The rate of population between the number of dogs and the number of cats is that the dog is greater than the cats.*

These sentences were written by students (one senior secondary and two tertiary) who were trying to describe a simple diagram showing *six dogs for every cat*. It is evident that they are unsure of the standard meanings of *amount* (versus *number*), *margin*, *rate* (*ratio?*), and *that* (versus *than*). These and other samples of written work from students reveal a poorly-developed grasp of fundamental mathematical concepts as well as inadequate English skills for the communication of mathematical ideas.

However, as Orr (1987) found in her work with students speaking Black English vernacular, continued practice at writing definitions and explanations enabled such students to gain control of the features of standard English, particularly prepositions, necessary for success in senior levels of mathematics and science.

Summary

It is now recognised that teachers of all subjects must become aware of the language demands of their fields. A mathematics curriculum needs to be one that extends students' mastery of analytic reading skills and of the language register used by mathematicians. Responsibility for teaching students how to read mathematical text **and** how to express mathematical information in writing must be accepted by mathematics teachers.

References

Bever, T.G. (1970) 'The cognitive basis for linguistic structures' in J.R. Hayes (Ed.), *Cognition and the development of language* Wiley, New York, (pp. 279–362).

Clements, M.A. (1984) 'Language factors in school mathematics' in P.Costello, S. Ferguson, K. Slinn, M. Stephens, D. Trembath, & D. Williams, (Eds.), *Facets of Australian Mathematics Education* Australian Association of Mathematics Teachers, (pp. 137–148).

Corson, D. (1989) 'Critical language awareness and the schools', *Vox. The Journal of the Australian Advisory Council on Languages and Multicultural Education 2*, (pp. 53–63).

Forster, K.I. (1979) 'Levels of processing and the structure of the language processor' in W.E. Cooper & E.C.T. Walker, (Eds.), *Sentence processing: psycholinguistic studies presented to Merrill Garrett* Erlbaum, Hillsdale, NJ, (pp. 27–85).

Lo Bianco, J. (1987) *National policy on languages* AGPS, Canberra.

Orr, E.W. (1987) *Twice as less* Norton, New York.

Smith, F. (1986) *Writing and the writer* Hillsdale, NJ: L. Erlbaum.

Trudgill, P. (1975) *Accent, dialect and the school* Edward Arnold, London.

Wanner, E. & Maratsos, M. (1978) 'An ATN approach to comprehension' in M. Halle, J. Bresnan, & G. Miller, (Eds.), *Linguistic theory and psychological reality* MIT Press, Cambridge, Mass, (pp. 119–161).

Bibliography

Burton, G.M. (1985) 'Writing as a way of knowing in a mathematics education class', *Arithmetic Teacher*, 33, (pp. 40–45).

Dale, T.C. & Cuevas G.J. (1987) 'Integrating language and mathematics learning' in J. Crandall, (Ed.), *ESL through content-area instruction – mathematics, science, social studies* Prentice Hall, Englewood Cliffs, NJ, (pp. 9–54).

Geeslin, W.E. (1977) 'Using writing about mathematics as a teaching technique', *Mathematics Teacher, 70(2)*, (pp. 117–119).

Keith, S.Z. (1988) 'Explorative writing and learning mathematics'. *Mathematics Teacher, 81(9)*, (pp. 714–719).

MacGregor, M.E. (in press) 'Psycholinguistic barriers to mathematical literacy' in R. Hunting, (Ed.), *Language issues in the learning and teaching of mathematics*. La Trobe University: Institute of Mathematics Education, Melbourne.

MacGregor, M.E. (1989) 'Reading and writing mathematics' *Australian Journal of Reading, 12(2)*, (pp. 153–161).

Matthews, P. (1988) *Language development and mathematics education: the learning of elementary algebra*. Paper presented at the Sixth International Congress on Mathematical Education, Budapest.

Pengelly, H. (1988) 'Representing mathematics: from materials to symbols' in D. Plummer, (Ed.), *Planning for thinkers and learners: the early years* Australian Reading Association, Melbourne (pp. 89–107).

Watson, M. (1980) 'Writing has a place in a mathematics class', *Mathematics Teacher, 73(7)*, (pp. 518–519).

Waywood, A. (in press) 'Mathematics and language: reflections on students using mathematics journals' in R. Hunting, (Ed.), *Language issues in the learning and teaching of mathematics*. La Trobe University: Institute of Mathematics Education, Melbourne.

9

The role of challenges

Rex Stoessiger and Joy Edmunds

Stoessiger and Edmunds acknowledge the need for natural language learning conditions to be present in mathematical classrooms. Their action-research with teachers indicates that when open-ended challenges are set in place in the classroom, then children are able to develop their own theories of the mathematical patterns in their lives. The use of challenges works because of the risk-free environment that teachers create, in which the learners have an opportunity to come to their own understandings and gradually refine their responses.

The lesson from language learning

In previous articles (Stoessiger and Edmunds, 1987; Stoessiger, 1988; Stoessiger and Edmunds, 1989) we have described how incongruities between the teaching of mathematics and the teaching of language led us, and the teachers we have worked with, to develop a new approach to teaching and learning mathematics. This approach is modelled on one increasingly being used for language. The language approach is described by *The Pathways of Language Development* (Education Department of Tasmania, 1987) in the following way:

> *The growing awareness that language learning is a wholistic, natural process, a constant construction of meaning by the learner, has highlighted the importance of what we know about children's oral acquisition as the basis for providing similar, more natural learning environments in which they will start to read and write at school.*

Our goal could well be described as adding 'and learn mathematics' to the sentiments of this statement, while recognising that this starts long before children come to school.

The words we would particularly highlight from the quote are, *natural process, wholistic, construction of meaning* and *natural learning environments* with the addition of the word *challenge*.

Specifically, we have been investigating how students might learn mathematics by a wholistic, natural process, where they are challenged to construct and refine their own meanings in a more natural learning environment.

Natural learning environments

We have previously described in detail how natural learning conditions as formalised by Brian Cambourne (1986) (and used as a basis of many current language programs) can be adapted by teachers for mathematics teaching and learning (see references above). We will not re-present this work here but must emphasise that we see the use of natural learning conditions as a very important way in which teachers can reconstitute their teaching of mathematics.

However, teachers have found that it is very difficult to implement natural learning conditions for mathematics if it is presented to students in conventional ways. In particular the use of open-ended problems, or challenges, has proved to be invaluable. It is challenges and why we see them as important for learning mathematics that form the subject of this paper.

What are challenges?

A challenge is an open-ended problem which a learner finds challenging, such as:

> *Some people say that to add 4 consecutive numbers you add the first and the last and multiply by two. What can you find out about this? Select your most interesting finding and display it.*

Challenges help learners construct their own mathematical ideas. Their open-ended nature allows learners to respond in ways which fit in with their own theories and to develop these theories further as a result. The teacher designs the challenge with the hope that it will challenge particular ideas held by particular students but learners make them their own as they respond. Typical challenges are shown in Figure 1.

Theoretical foundations

Our philosophical position is that learners have their own theories which they test by trying them out in the world. Even very young

Fig. 1: Typical challenges

- Use pipe cleaners to make angles of very different sizes. What triangles can you make with your angles? Record something interesting you find out about the angles that make triangles.

- Write down the three times table. What patterns can you find? Select the most interesting for display.

- Make something to measure angles with. Use it to find out about the angles in your classroom. Report your most useful finding.

from Stoessiger, R. & Edmunds, J. (1989)

learners are developing coherent groups of ideas about the meanings of words, the people around them and the repeating patterns in their lives. They act on the basis of these developing theories.

We have developed these views into an educational theory with the help of the work of Walker, Keoh and Boud (1985). Walker argues that all our knowledge is theory: *'our basic items of knowledge are not particular data, intuitions or statements, but whole theories'* (p. 56). He asserts that all we have are theories and that there are no 'facts' or *a priori* knowledge which can provide secure foundations for the rest of our knowledge. In Walker's view, itself a theory which he calls one of *'materialistic pragmatism'*, the acceptance of a theory does not hinge on its provability but rather on its coherence with all our other theories and on its capability to solve problems in the present historical context. The first requirement is wholistic, the second, pragmatic.

In considering materialist pragmatism in an educational context the focus shifts from the theories that learners have to questions of their improvement. We have suggested that learning can be seen as a process of **theory refinement** (Stoessiger and Felton, 1988). In a theory refinement approach learners are challenged to test their theories both in terms of their coherence and their practical problem solving capacity.

These views are similar to those forming the theory of constructivism, particularly as it has been developed in a mathematical context (von

Glasersfeld, 1984; Cobb, Wood and Yackel, in press). The constructivist position is that students are active makers of their own mathematical understandings:

> *The currently held view of cognitively-orientated researchers in general and those specifically interested in children's learning of mathematics is one in which students are active participants as they construct knowledge by reorganising their current ways of knowing. Children learn on the basis of their experiences as they interact in their physical and social environment and new learning occurs when current ideas give rise to problematic situations and new ideas are constructed to restore coherence and meaning to experience.*

(Wood, Cobb and Yackel, 1989)

Clearly constructivism and theory refinement have much in common. Specifically, they both focus on the active involvement of learners in developing their own ideas, that these ideas are to be tested in the learner's environment and need to be coherent and meaningful.

Our particular orientation towards constructivism is to focus on the theories that learners hold and how they can be improved. We would like to ensure that those theories are challenged as part of the refinement processes operating within an environment where natural learning conditions have been established.

Refinement processes and the importance of meaning

Refinement processes are central to children's learning before they come to school. Adults expect children to 'have a go' but they don't require them to get it right at the first attempt. Language develops as the child makes a rough approximation, and is positively rewarded. The first time a child says 'da' for 'daddy' there is great excitement and the child is accordingly rewarded. Counting develops similarly as the child repeats a sequence of number names in response to a collection of objects and the adults respond positively. Adults are often pleased with very young children even if the numbers are not in the conventional order.

> Child: *'One, seven, two, three.'*
> Adult: *'Yes dear that's good counting.'*

The adult response is entirely appropriate. The young child is approximating counting behaviour even though the order is not yet correct. Of course the adult may well go on to model the conventional counting order but there is no expectation that the child will quickly adopt it. Parents know well that it takes many, many demonstrations and plenty of time for experimentation before children start to say the names in the conventional order and associate them with single objects. Refinement processes are increasingly becoming part of language learning in schools. Students are not expected to write perfectly at the first attempt. The most important thing is that they write. This is then treated as a first draft and, when appropriate, is refined. The spelling is checked, punctuation added and the style and grammar improved. Of course teachers convey their expectations that students will come to adopt conventional forms, to spell correctly and to express themselves well. They may even demonstrate more conventional approaches back to the student if that seems desirable. But all this is in the context of the student being praised for writing, however approximately, in the first instance. The only reservation is that the writing must make sense. If that is not the case the teacher may be quite unaccepting. After all the point of any language work is to convey meaning.

We advocate the use of open-ended problems, or challenges, because they allow refinement processes to operate for mathematics. If the mathematics can be presented in an open-ended way, students can make a first response which can then be used as a basis for refinement. If the task is genuinely open-ended a teacher can readily accept the student's response as a first attempt and respond favourably. This is often not the case with closed problems where the inevitable adult response is a negative one if the answer is incorrect. The response is negative because incorrect mathematics lacks meaning and mathematics is just as much about conveying meaning as is language.

The response to a challenge will reflect the students' mathematical theories and their attempts to convey meaning. Sometimes the responses will contain numerical inaccuracies so in the refinement stages students need to check their calculations to ensure they are accurate. Sometimes students will use long-winded methods which can be improved. Often the theories themselves need improvement.

Most of us do our initial mathematical work in 'back-of-an-envelope' style (MacGregor, this issue). It is important to follow through the thinking without getting distracted by the need for special setting out. We can only concentrate on so much at a time. But if that mathematics is to be communicated to someone else it needs to be well set out. Hence the importance of refinement processes in teaching students the need for setting out as part of preparing mathematics for communication to others. Adding a diagram or graphical representation may also make the mathematics more understandable. Hence this may be an important part of the refinement processes for mathematics analogous to adding an illustration to a piece of writing.

Challenges: revealing students' thinking

Open-ended situations allow students to demonstrate what they are comfortable with and which theories they need to develop further. When teachers first introduce challenges into their classrooms students are usually cautious. They may not believe that they can't get the mathematics wrong! They often respond by playing it safe and revealing only the mathematics they are comfortable with. Of course this is useful information for the teacher.

As students become used to challenges they usually become more adventuresome. Sometimes they need encouragement from the teacher. It is important for students to know they are expected to take risks and that the teacher will appreciate their attempts. As their confidence develops students start to operate with bigger or different numbers, to tackle challenges in more creative ways and to go deeper in their explorations. As a result the teacher comes to see more of their thinking. Quite often teachers discover that students can do much more than was expected of them. Young students may show they are quite capable of working with large numbers, others start dealing with decimals and negative numbers well before the curriculum guides would suggest.

Thus misconceptions also become apparent. It may be seeing a student write 10010 for a hundred and ten or hearing someone say that 0.5 plus 0.5 is 'zero point ten'. These are just as useful to the teacher. Not as mistakes to be corrected, although it may be appropriate to model the conventional usage without depreciating the student's work. Their main value is the opportunity they give for teachers to challenge students to refine their ideas. The student who records a hundred and ten as 10010 might be challenged to write number sentences involving 100 using a calculator. The 'zero point ten' student might be challenged to add fractions and their decimal equivalents using fraction strips and to look for patterns.

Challenges: individualising the learning

Challenges allow students to individualise the work for themselves. They respond at their own level. This is a real advantage for teachers because a few challenges can replace a large number of work sheets. Many teachers start a new section of the curriculum with a very open challenge so that the whole class can respond at their own level. After seeing how individuals respond the teacher may then develop more specific challenges designed for particular groups of students.

With challenges there is more room for error than with conventional attempts to individualise the curriculum. As long as the new activities are still open-ended students will again respond at their own level.

A particular challenge is useful while it remains challenging. Hence challenges can be re-used with the same group of students, allowing them to explore them more deeply. Many teachers have a 'used' challenge board, or box, in the classroom where they store challenges for later use.

Challenges: developing positive attitudes

One of the problems with conventional, right-wrong mathematics problems is that students either find them too easy or else get a considerable proportion wrong. Either way negative attitudes to the subject may build up over a period of time. Most people leave the subject when they are no longer succeeding and as a result community attitudes to the subject are quite negative. To ensure that students generally succeed, teachers break the subject down into a sequence of small steps. This is not all that successful in practice because if a student fails to grasp one step then learning subsequent steps may be very difficult. As well, the reduction of the subject into fragments results in each component becoming quite remote from real world mathematical problems which come in wholes rather than as fragments. Students perceive the difference between school mathematics and the real world again and their attitudes suffer. Challenges provide a way out of these difficulties: if they are genuinely open-ended, students can always succeed at their own level; if they are genuinely challenging students can explore them at more difficult levels. They present wholistic mathematical situations, not fragments.

Conclusion

We have indicated the main reasons why we believe that the use of challenges can change the teaching of mathematics for the better. We would add one additional reason. Challenges are fun. Both teachers and students enjoy challenges in the classroom.

NOTE: Published sets of challenge cards are now available from the Australian Association of Mathematics Teachers, and through local State associations, or from the authors at CDE Section, Education Department of Tasmania, 71 Letitia St, North Hobart 7000.

References

Cambourne, B. (1988) *The Whole Story: Natural Learning and the Acquisition of Literacy in the Classroom*. Ashton Scholastic, Gosford Australia.

Cobb, P. (1989) Personal communication.

Cobb, P., Wood, T. and Yackel, E. (in press) 'Classrooms as Learning Environments for Teachers and Researchers', *Journal for Research in Mathematics Education Monograph*.

Education Department of Tasmania (1987) *The Pathways of Language Development*, Hobart.

Stoessiger, R. (1988) *Using Language Learning Conditions in Mathematics*, PEN 68. Newtown, Australia, PETA.

Stoessiger, R. and Edmunds, J. (1987) *Investigating a Process Approach to Mathematics*, Education Department of Tasmania, Hobart.

Stoessiger, R. and Edmunds, J. (1989) 'Metaphors for Mathematics', *Australian Journal of Reading*, 12, (p. 123).

Stoessiger, R. and Felton, H. (1988) 'Theory Refinement: A Practical Way of Linking Research to Practice and Policy Making', Paper presented to AARE Conference, Armidale, 1988.

von Glasersfeld, E. (1984) 'An Introduction to Radical Constructivism' in P. Watzlawick (Ed.), *The Invented Reality* Norton, New York.

Wood, T., Cobb, P. and Yackel, E. (in press) 'The Contextual Nature of Teaching: Change in Mathematics but Stability in Reading', *Elementary School Journal*.

Walker D., Keoh, R., Boud, D. (Eds.) (1985) *Turning Experience into Learning*, Kogan Page, London.

Recording Methods

Hop		hop	ㄴ
Side Step		s p 2	◁ →
Jump		i c p	⬍